This book is a gift not only to the world, but to CMJ as a new Publishers. I have prayed to Our Mother to allow me to be able to contribute to her work, and this I believe is an answer to that prayer. I have been to Medjugorje twice, but have never really taken the time to review these messages until Father Becker and I undertook the joy of doing this book. They truly answer your concerns and direct you to the correct path to follow for total conversion.

Please invoke the assistance of the Holy Spirit when you read these messages. Please take the time and meditate on one message at a time. Do it daily in the morning and it will help to keep you in prayer for that day.

Jim Gilboy
Publisher

DEDICATION

*To all the Priests of the World
and in a special way to
all the Priests of the
Archdiocese of Chicago.*

FOREWARD

This book seeks to make available the messages of Our Lady. The Gospa (in Croatian), the Blessed Virgin Mary, the Mother of Our Lord and Saviour Jesus Christ, given at Medjugorje in Bosnia-Hercegovina to six visionaries beginning on June 25, 1981. There are many books written about the messages. One well known and dedicated priest in Our Lady's Work is Franciscan Friar, Fr. Slavko Barbaric. His many prayer books and commentaries are truly beautiful and useful in helping to deepen our faith and prayer life and to better understand Our Lady's Work in Medjugorje. Fr. Rene Laurentina has a wonderful book that discerns the authenticity of the apparitions entitled *Is the Virgin Mary Appearing at Medjugorje?*, by The Word Among Us Press, Washington, D.C., 1984.

This little book, however, simply seeks to bring together Our Lady's words over the years, to make them easily available so her request to "spread the messages" might be better accomplished. So too, this little book is left without commentary so that one may allow Our Lady to speak directly to one's own heart, mind and soul. She is the Mother of Jesus and Our Mother, Jesus' last gift given to us at the foot of the Cross when He said to John, ". . . Behold your Mother." She is the Mother of us all, reversing the role of Eve, the first mother of the living, who sinned. mary who in her Immaculate Conception was preserved by grace from the Original Sin of Adam and Eve, is the New Eve, the Mother of Our Saviour and now Our Mother, the Mother of all God's children on earth. In her Motherly role, she desires to speak to all of us, not just Catholics, not only Christians, but all people, all her children redeemed by her Son. These messages of hers are a call to all humanity to return to God their Creator.

May the belief in the Resurrection of Jesus Christ help you to trust in the ever present reality of God and all the Angels and Saints in Heaven. May we all be open to their assistance in helping poor humanity find the source of Peace once again! Mary, the Queen of Peace leads us to True Peace, her Son Jesus, Who is the Way, the Truth and the Life—the Prince of

Peace! Mary, Our Mother, is calling us all. She is calling to you!

Father Charles Becker
Chicago, Illinois

INTRODUCTION

The Church in her Wisdom often times moves slowly in pronouncing judgments on matter of private revelation. Such is the case in Medjugorje, Bosnia-Hercegovina, where it is believed that six visionaries, one child and five teenagers, on June 25, 1981, began conversing with Jesus' Mother, the Blessed Virgin Mar. Three of these six along with two others, first experienced an apparition of the Blessed Mother the day before, June 24, 1981, the Feast day of the Birth of St. John the Baptist, however, it was a silent apparition. Four of the six visionaries continue to see and speak with her every day! The Church, in its role as guardian of souls, seeks to safeguard her children from anything that could harm their journey to eternal life. Therefore, trusting in Jesus' Church and the Vicar He has appointed to the Chair of St. Peter, Pope John Paul II, we humbly submit to the final decision of the Magisterium of the

Catholic Church, regarding the apparitions in Medjugorje. To date, the Church has not found anything contrary to it Teachings. Therefore, since there has been no official pronouncement either positively or negatively regarding the supernatural reality of this matter, one is free to believe in them, in accordance with the decree of Pope Urban VIII.

Medjugorje has become an international center of prayer, so affirmed by the Commission of Bishops of former Yugoslavia that have overseen the events at Medjugorje. It has become a place of devotion and conversion of heart. Our Lady has told the visionaries that these are her last appearances on earth. She has come to tell us that "God exists." Before her last appearance she has promised to leave a visible sign on the mountain where the first apparition took place so that all may believe.

The messages are often summarized by the visionaries in 5 points and convey to the world an urgent need for:

1. *Faith*—Belief and trust in God.
2. *Conversion*—Commitment to God. Let God rule your life. Turn away from sin.

3. *Prayer*—Regular Mass, monthly confession, daily rosary and reading the Bible. Consecration to the Sacred Heart of Jesus and the Immaculate Heart of Mary.

4. *Penance and Fasting*—Bread and water on Fridays (and Wednesdays) if you can. Practice other self-denial if unable to fast.

5. *Peace*—Pray for peace in your heart, peace in your family and for peace in the world. "The most important message is peace. She insisted on that."—visionary Vicka Ivankovic, *Is the Virgin Mary Appearing in Medjugorje?* by Fr. Rene Laurentina, p. 5.

Close to 30 million people from all over the world have been to Medjugorje since the apparitions began. These millions have been touched by Our Lady's presence there and her urgent messages. Her call to pray and to spread her messages have brought many to a conversion of heart (a reawakened love for God) and a desire to help others find the same. Our simple and complete "yes" to Our Lady, like her total surrendering "Yes" to God, is the beginning of this conversion, this reawakened faith, love and peace of God in the heart.

May your "yes" to God through saying "yes" to Our Lady, bring peace and understanding of God's Will and Plan for you!

The messages in this book begin with March 1, 1984, and are intended for the world. At that time, the messages were given weekly to the visionary Maria Pavlovic. The messages before that time were meant only for the visionaries and the people of their parish. We have included a short history that comes from the Medjugorje computer web site of these early messages to help you achieve a fuller understanding of Our Lady's coming. On January 8, 1987, Maria began receiving these messages once a month instead of weekly and they have been given on the 25th of each month ever since! Thanks be to God! Thank you Mary!

The messages of Our Lady used in this book are from the English translation sent out by St. James Church in Medjugorje. Father Miljenko Stojic, O.F.M., who publishes the Medjugorje Press Bulletin in Medjugorje for the internet, in Mary 1997, was very encouraging regarding this effort to publish the messages in English.

he said it is important to help spread the messages and he offered some suggestions from the Croatian books already in print. Future editions of this book will include the latest messages. We hopefully will have supplemental editions of the messages of Our Lady in Medjugorje between publications.

Father Charles Becker
and
CMJ Marian Publishers
P.O. Box 661
Oak Lawn, Illinois 60454
www.cmjbooks.com

O. A

P- • • • • • • • • • • • • • • •

STATEMENT ON PRIVATE REVELATIONS

The words of the Second Vatican Council in the Document "The Dogmatic Constitution on the Church" (Lumen Gentium), Chapter II No. 12 helps us to understand the spiritual realities we speak of:

"The Holy Spirit . . . distributes special graces among the faithful of every rank . . . These charismatic gifts, whether they be the most outstanding or the more simple and widely diffused, are to be received with thanksgiving and consolation, for they are exceedingly suitable and useful for the needs of the Church. . . . Judgment as to their genuineness and proper use belongs to those who preside over the Church, and to whose special competence it belongs, no indeed to extinguish the Spirit, but to test all things and hold fast to that which is good (cf. Th 5:12, 19-21)."—*The Documents of Vatican II*, editors Abbott and Gallagher.

His Holiness, Pope Urban VIII, (1623-44) also sheds spiritual light on these matters in his often quoted statement: "In cases which concern private revelations, it is better to believe than not to believe, for, if you believe, and it is proven true, you will be happy that you have believed, . . . if you believe, and it should be proven false, you will receive all blessing as if it had been true, because you believed it to be true."

Unless an apparition site has been condemned by the church, (meaning the local bishop), then the faithful are fee to follow an unapproved apparition. However, caution and discernment must be exercised to avoid following false mystical experiences and potential harm. Let us remember that the "Miracle of the Sun" at Fatima on October 13, 1917, occurred before the Church had accepted or approved those most significant apparitions. If everyone would have waited for approval then no one would have seen the miracle! What is needed is faith and trust! Again, we still need to be careful when approaching "new" mystical realities that are not approved, "seeking counsel from every wise man" (Tobit 4:18a), lest we be led into confusion or darkness, which is where Satan would want to lead us.

Fr. Charles Becker

A SHORT HISTORY OF OUR LADY'S APPARITIONS IN MEDJUGORJE

For quite a while now, in Medjugorje (Citluk, Bosnia-Hercegovina) six trustworthy witnesses, testify firmly under oath, that since the 24th of June 1981, the Blessed Virgin mary, or the "Gospa," as she is affectionately known as here, appears to them every day up to the present.

The first day

On the said date at approximately six o'clock in the evening, on the area of Crnica hill known as Podbrdo, the children, Ivanka Ivankovic, Mirjana Dragicevic, Vicka Ivankovic, Ivan Dragicevic, Ivan Ivankovic and Milka Pavlovic saw an incredible beautiful young woman with a little child in her arms.

She didn't say anything to them but indicated with gestures that they should come closer. Surprised and frightened they were afraid to come near, even though they immediately thought her to be Our Lady.

The second day

On the second day, the 25th of June 1981, the children agreed to meet once again at the same place that Our Lady had previously appeared, in the hope of seeing her again. All of a sudden there was a flash of light. The children looked up and saw Our Lady, this time without a child. She was smiling and joyful and was indescribably beautiful. With her hands she gestured to them to come closer. The children braced themselves and went up to her. They immediately fell to their knees and began to pray the "Our Father, Hail Mary and Glory Be." Our Lady prayed together with them except for when they prayed the "Hail Mary."

After the prayer she began to speak with the children, Ivanka, first of all, asked her about her mother who died two months previously. And

Mirjana asked Our Lady for some sign to be given to show to the people that they were neither lying nor crazy, as some people had said.

Our Lady finally left the children with the words, "God be with you my angels!" Before that, when the children asked her if they would see her the following day, she replied by nodding her head.

According to the visionaries the whole encounter was indescribable. On that day two of the children which made up the previous group were missing: Ivan Ivankovic and Milka Pavlovic. They were replaced by two others, Maria Pavlovic and Jokov Colo. And from that day onwards according to these six children, Our Lady regularly appears to them. Milka Pavlovic and Ivan Ivankovic, who were present on the first day of apparitions, did not see Our Lady again, even though they returned to the apparition site, in the hope of seeing her.

The third day

On the 26th of June, the children full of anticipation waited at around six o'clock, which was when she previously appeared. They were going towards the same place, to meet her there. They were very happy, although their joy was mixed with fear wondering what would be the outcome of all this. Despite all this, the children could feel some sort of inner strength attracting them to meet with Our Lady.

Suddenly, while the children were still on their way a light flashed three times. To them and to those following them, it was a sign indicating Our Lady's whereabouts. On that third day Our Lady appeared even higher up than on the previous days. All at once Our Lady disappeared. But when the children began to pray, she reappeared. She was cheerful and smiling serenely and once again her beauty was overwhelming.

As they left their houses some older women advised them to carry holy water with them to make sure that it was not of satan. When they were with Our Lady Vicka took the water and splashed it in the direction of the vision saying, "If you are Our Blessed Mother, please stay, and if you are not, go away from us." Our Lady smiled at this and remained with the children.

Then Mirjana asked her name and she replied, "I am the Blessed Virgin Mary."

On the same day, coming down Podbrdo, Our Lady appeared one more time, this time however only to Maria saying, "Peace, peace, peace, and only peace." Behind her, Maria could see a cross. After which Our Lady repeated, in tears, the following words, "Peace must reign between man and God, and between all people!" The area where this took place is about half way up to the Apparition Site.

The fourth day

On the 27th of June Our Lady appeared three times to the children. On that occasion the children asked all kinds of questions and Our Lady responded. For priests, she gave this message, "May the priests firmly believe and may they take care of the faith of the people!" Once again, Jakov and Mirjana asked for a sign, because the people had begun to accuse them of lying and of taking drugs. "Do not be afraid of anything," Our Lady replied.

Before parting, when asked if she would

come again, she indicated that she would. On the way down Podbrdo, Our Lady appeared one more time to say goodbye with the words, "May God be with you my angels, to in peace!"

The fifth day

On the 28th of June big crowds were gathering from all parts even from the early hours of the morning. By noon there were about fifteen thousand people. On the same day, the Parish Priest, F. Jozo Zovko, examined the children on what they had seen and heard in the previous days.

At. the usual time Our Lady appeared again. The children prayed with her, and afterwards they questioned her. Vicka, for example, asked, "My dear Lady, what do you want from us and what do you want from our priests?" Our Lady replied, "The people should pray and firmly believe." Regarding priests, she replied that they should believe firmly and help others to do the same.

On that day Our Lady came and went many times. During one of those times the children asked her why she doesn't appear in the Parish Church for everyone to see. She replied, "Blessed are those who have not seen and yet believe."

Even though the crowds were pushing them with their questions and curiosities, and the day was heavy and sultry, the children felt as though they were in heaven.

The sixth day

On the 29th of June the children were taken to Mostar fro a medical examination after which they were proclaimed "healthy." The statement of the head doctor was, "The children aren't crazy, the person who brought them here must be though . . ."

The crowds on Apparition Hill that day were greater than ever. As soon as the children arrived at the usual place and began to pray, Our Lady appeared. On that occasion the Blessed Mother exhorted them to have faith saying, "The people should believe firmly and have no fear."

On that day, a doctoress who was following

and observing them, during the apparition desired to touch Our Lady. The children guided her hand to the place where Our Lady's shoulder was, and she felt a tingling sensation. The doctor, even though an atheist had to admit that, "Here, something strange is happening!"

On that same day a child by the name of Daniel Setka was miraculously healed. Her parents had brought her to Medjugorje, praying specifically for a healing. Our Lady had promised that his would come about if the parents prayed and fasted and strongly believed. The child thereupon was healed.

The seventh day

On the 30th of June two young girls suggested to the children to go by car further away to be able to stroll in peace. Really their intention was to bring them away from the area and keep them until after the normal apparition time had passed. However, even though the children were far away from Podbrdo, at the usual time of the apparition, it was as if an interior call prompted them to ask to be let out of the car. As soon as they did, and said a prayer, Our Lady drew near to them, from the direction of Podbrdo which was now over a kilometer away. She prayed seven "Our Fathers," etc. And so the girls' trick had no effect. Soon after this the police began to hinder the children and the pilgrims going on Podbrdo; the site of apparitions. The children, and soon afterwards even the crowds were forbidden to go there. But Our Lady continued to appear to them in secret places, in their homes and in the fields. The children had already gained confidence, and openly spoke with Our Lady, eagerly seeking her advice, listening to her warnings and messages. The events of Medjugorje continued in this fashion up until the 15th of January, 1982.

In the meantime, the parish priest began to host the pilgrims in the Church, enabling them to participate in the rosary and to celebrate the Eucharist. The children also gave out the rosary Our Lady sometimes appeared to them in the church at that time. Even the parish priest himself once while praying the rosary, saw Our Lady. Immediately he broke off praying and spontaneously started to sing a popular hymn, "lijepa si, lijepa Djevo Mario";—"O how beautiful you are Most Blessed Virgin Mary." The whole church could see that something unusual was happening to him. Afterwards he stated that he had seen her. And so, he who up until then had not only been doubtful, but openly against such rumors of the apparitions, became their defender. He testified his support of the apparitions even to the point of serving a prison sentence.

From the 15th of January 1982 onwards the children saw Our Lady in a closed off area of the Parish Church. The Parish Priest arranged this because of the newly arisen difficulties and sometimes even dangers which provided themselves for the visionaries. Previously the children had ensured that this was in accord with Our Lady's wishes. Because of the prohibition of the Diocesan Bishop however, from April 1985 onwards the children ceased to use the area of the church as an apparition site. Instead, they went to a room in the Parish house.

All this time, from the beginning of the apparitions up until today, there have only been five days when none of the children saw Our Lady.

Our Lady didn't always appear in the same place either, nor to the same group. nor individuals, nor did her apparitions always last a specified period. Sometimes the apparitions lasted two minutes, sometimes an hour. Neither did Our Lady appear at the children's will. Sometimes they prayed and waited but Our Lady didn't appear until a little while afterwards,, unexpectedly and unforwarned. And sometimes she appeared to one and not to the others. If she hadn't promised an appointed time, nobody knew when she would appear, or if she would appear. Neither did she appear always to just the aforesaid visionaries, but to others also of different age, stature, race, education and walks of life. All this suggests that the apparitions are not a product of the imagination. It depends neither on time nor place, nor desire nor the prayer of pilgrim or visionary, but moreover on the will of He who permits it.

MESSAGES

According to the united testimony of the visionaries, Our Lady on the occasion of her apparition gave a series of messages, to be transmitted to the people. Even though there are many messages, they can however be summarized in five themes, because all the messages basically underline or lead up to these five.

General Overview of the messages

PEACE—Already on the third day, Our Lady stressed peace as the first of her messages: "Peace, peace, peace and only peace!" after which she said twice, "Peace must reign between God and man and between people." Considering that maria could see a cross, when Our Lady gave this message, the obvious conclusion is that this peace comes from God. God, who through Our Lady in Christ became our peace. "(Ephesians 2:14) "For He is the peace between us . . ." This peace, "the world cannot give" (John 14:27) and that's why Christ commanded His apostles to bring it to

12

the world (Matthew 10:11) so that all men could become "sons of peace" (Luke 10:6). That's why Our Lady as "Queen of Apostles" in Medjugorje specifically refers to herself as "Queen of Peace." Who better than she, can more successfully convince today's world, which is faced with the threat of destruction, how great and how necessary peace is.

FAITH—The second of Our Lady's messages is faith. Already on the fourth, fifth and sixth day of apparitions, Our Lady exhorted those present to have strong faith. Understandably, she repeated this message many times. Without faith we cannot arrive at peace! Not only this but faith is itself an answer to God's Word, which He not only proclaims but actually gives to us. When we believe, we accept God's Word which in Christ, became "our peace" (Ephesians 2:14). Accepting it, the individual becomes a new creature, with a new life of Christ within, and a share in God's nature (1 Peter 1:4, Ephesians 2:18). In this way the individual ensured peace with God and with others.

Once again there is no one who can better understand the necessity and efficaciousness of faith than Our Lady. That's why she stressed it on every occasion and charged the visionaries to bring the light of faith to others. Our Lady presented faith as an answer to everything, no matter whatever people were looking for. She presented it as the prerequisite of all prayer, desires and demands, relating it to health, wholeness and to all other human necessities.

CONVERSION—Conversion was, another one of Our Lady's frequent messages. This presupposes that she noticed either a weakness or a complete lack of faith in humanity today. And without conversion it is impossible to achieve peace. true conversion mans, the purifying or cleansing of the heart, (Jeremiah 4:14), because a corrupt or "deteriorated" heart is the basis of bad relations, which in turn brings social disorder, unjust laws, base constitutions, etc. Without a radical change of heart, without the conversion of the heart, there is no peace. For this reason, Our Lady continually suggests frequent confession. The request is directed to all without differentiation because, "not one of us is just . . . all have wandered, not one does right" (Romans 3:11-12).

PRAYER—Almost daily, from the fifth day of apparitions onwards Our Lady recommends prayer. She request everyone to "pray without ceasing" just as Christ himself taught (Mark 9:29, Matthew 9:38, Luke 11:5-13). Prayer, therefore, stimulates and strengthens our faith, without which our relationship with God is disordered—as is our relationship with each other. Prayer also reminds us of how close God is to us even in our daily lives: In prayer we acknowledge Him, we give Him thanks for His gifts to us, and we are filled with a hopeful expectancy of that which we need, but particularly our redemption. Prayer solidifies the equilibrium of the individual, and aids us in our "ordered relationship with God," without which it is impossible to maintain peace either with God or with our neighbor.

The Word of the Lord acquainted itself with all humanity and awaits humanity's response. It is precisely this which gives prayer its "justification." Our response should be "spoken faith," or "prayer." In prayer, faith animates, renews, strengthens and sustains itself. In addition to this, man's prayer really bears witness to the Gospel, and to the existence of God, thus provoking a response of faith in others.

FASTING—Already on the sixth day of the apparitions. Our Lady often recommended fasting because it aids faith. That is, the practice of fasting aids and ensures control over oneself. Only the person who can dominate himself is truly free, and is capable of abandoning himself to god and to his neighbor, as faith demands. Fasting guarantees him that his abandonment to faith is secure and sincere. It helps him to free himself from every slavery, but especially from the slavery to sin. Whoever is not in the possession of oneself is in some way enslaved. Therefore, fasting helps the individual to restrain himself from disordered pleasure-seeking which in turn leads him to a futile and useless existence often wasteful of the very goods which are necessary to other just for basic survival.

With fasting we also retrieve the gift which creates within us a realistic love for the poor and the destitute, which up to a certain point eases the difference between rich and poor. It therefore heals the wants of the poor and also heals the excesses and overindulgence of others. And in its own way, it gives a dimension of peace which today in a special way, is threatened by the difference in the lifestyles of the rich and the poor (e.g., North and South).

To sum up, we can say that Our Lady's messages underline that peace is the greatest good, and that faith, conversion, prayer and fasting are the means by which we can attain it.

Special Messages

Outside of the five messages which, as we have said are the important messages which Our Lady immediately gave to the whole world, she started from the 1st of March 1984, every Thursday, mainly through the visionary Maria Pavlovic to give special messages to the Parish of Medjugorje and to the pilgrims who come. Our Lady therefore, outside of the six visionaries chose the parish of Medjugorje together with the pilgrims who come here to be her collaborators and witnesses. This is clear from the first of the Thursday messages, where she says: "I am choosing this parish in a special way and I want to guide it." She emphasized this once again when she said, "I am choosing this parish in a special way, which is dearer to me than others, where I joyfully went when the Almighty sent me" (25th March 1985). Our Lady gave a reason too for her choices saying: "Convert you in the Parish, this is my second wish. In that way, all those who come here will convert" (8th March 1984). "I am asking you, especially the members of this Parish, to live my messages" (16th August 1984). First of all the parishioners and the pilgrims should become witnesses of her apparitions, and her messages, so that we can then unite with her and the visionaries in the realization of her plan for conversion of the world and reconciliation with God.

Our Lady well knows the weakness and the nature of the parishioners and pilgrims with whom she wishes to collaborate in the salvation of the world. She is aware of the need for supernatural strength. That's why she leads them to the fount of that strength. This, primarily is prayer. She ardently and continuously exhorts us to pray. Of all prayer, she especially stresses the Holy Mass (7th March 1985; 16th May 1985), and recommends continuous devotion to the Blessed Sacrament (15th march 1984). She also encourages devotion to the Holy Spirit (2nd June 1984; 9th June 1984; 11th April 1985; 23rd May 1988, etc.) and the reading of the Sacred Scripture (8th September 1984; 14th February 1985).

With these special messages to the parish and its pilgrims, Our Lady wishes that the first messages, which in the beginning were intended for the whole world, are deepened, made more acceptable and understandable to others.

From the 25th of January 1987 Our Lady began to give the message on the 25th of every month instead of every Thursday, through the visionary Maria Pavlovic. This still continues today.

Fr. Ljudevit Rupcic
(Professor of Theology and translator of Sacred Scripture into the Croatian language. Fr. Rupcic is resident in Medjugorje.)

THE LAST OF MIRJANA DRAGICE-VIC'S DAILY MEETINGS WITH OUR LADY, CHRISTMAS 1982

The last day of my daily apparitions was on Christmas day, 25th of December 1982. Our Lady stayed with me for forty-five minutes on that occasion. For a month Our Lady had been preparing me for that meeting. She has been explaining everything to me in a motherly way. She told me that I had completed that which I had been necessary for. She told me that I must understand and am mature enough to turn back to normal daily living, like other girls of my age. I must continue to live without her motherly advice and without those very necessary conversations with her. She promised me that she would always be with me and that she would help me in the most difficult moments in life. For as long as I live with God, she will help me.

She told me that this would be the last of our daily meetings, but that she would leave me a gift, i.e., that for as long as I live, I would see her on my birthday.

This last meeting with Our Lady was very difficult for me. I cannot describe with words the pain that I felt in my soul knowing that I would no longer see her every day. It's as if, not so long ago, I received the most beautiful gift of my life, and that now I am losing it. Our Lady knew of my suffering and pain; and to cheer me up, she prayed with e and encouraged me to sing and praise God. I prayed the prayer that I always prayed, when I was alone with her, "Hail Holy Queen."

I will always remember her words, "I choose you, and I told you everything that is necessary. I entrusted you with the knowledge of abominations which you must carry within, with dignity. Think of me, and how much I too shed tears because of these. You must always be brave. you quickly understood my messages, and so you must understand that now I must leave. Be brave . . .!"

That which she said has remained with me, it was for me personally.

P.S. That first month was really difficult for me. Our Lady had warned me about that too. I fell into a deep state of depression. I escaped from everything. I closed myself up in my room, where Our Lady used to await me. I cried and called out to her. I felt her help and longed for my birthday . . .

Mirjana Dragicevic-Soldo

THE LAST OF IVANKA IVANKOVIC'S DAILY APPARITIONS AT MEDJUGORJE, 7TH MAY 1985

On the evening of the 6th of May 1985, Ivan, Jakov and Ivanka had their apparition. Their apparition lasted eight minutes, six minutes longer than the others. During this apparition, Our Lady gave Ivanka the tenth secret, finishing it with an account of the future of the world. Our Lady told her to await her alone the following day, without the other visionaries.

On the 7th of may 1985, Ivanka had an apparition in her home. Fr. Slavko Barbaric gave her paper on which she wrote:

Just as before, Our Lady came, she greeted me in the usual way saying, "Praised be Jesus!" and I answered her, "May Jesus and Mary forever be praised!" Never before had I seen such a beautiful Blessed Virgin Mary. She was so gentle and so beautiful! Today she had the most beautiful dress that I had ever seen in my life. The dress was shining in sliver and gold. Her veil and her crown were the same. There were two angels with her. They too were dressed like Our Lady. Both the angels and Our Lady were so beautiful that there are no words to describe them. It has to be experienced. Our Lady asked me if I had any particular wish. I asked her if I could see my earthly mother. Our Lady smiled and nodded her head. All of a sudden my mother was there. She was smiling. Our Lady told me to stand. I stood up. My mother hugged me and kissed me and said, "My child, I am so proud of you!" My Mother kissed me and then disappeared. After this, the

23

Blessed Virgin Mary said this: "My dear child, today is our last meeting, but do not be sad because I will come to you on every anniversary save this one. My child, do not think that you have done something wrong, and that that's why I no longer come. No, this isn't true. The plan which my Son and I have, you accepted with all your heart and completed your part. Be happy because I am your mother and I love you with all my heart. Ivanka, thank you for having responded to the invitation of my Son and for persevering and for always being close to Him and staying until He had completed that for which He asked of you. My child, tell your friends that both I and my Son will always be there for you when you seek or call us. That which I told you during these years about the secrets, it is still not time to tell anyone. Ivanka, the grace which you and the others received, nobody on this earth has received up until now!"

After these words, I asked Our Lady if I could kiss her.

She simply nodded her head. I kissed her. I asked for her blessing. She blessed me, smiled and said, "Go in the peace of God!"

She left slowly, and with her, the two angels left. The Blessed Virgin Mary was extremely happy. She remained with me one hour.

Ivanka Ivankovic-Elez

MESSAGES

March 1, 1984

"Dear children!

I have chosen this parish in a special way and I wish to lead it. I am guarding it in love an I want everyone to be mine. Thank you for having responded tonight. I wish you always to be with me and my Son in ever greater numbers. I shall speak a message to you every Thursday."

March 8, 1984

"Thank you for having responded to my call. Dear children, you in the parish, be converted. This is my other wish. That way, all those who shall come here shall be able to convert."

March 15, 1984

Tonight also, dear children, I am grateful to you in a special way for being here. Unceasingly, adore the Most Blessed Sacrament of the Altar. I am always present when the faithful are adoring. Special graces are then being received."

March 22, 1984

"Dear children!

In a special way this evening I am calling you during Lent to honor the wounds of my Son, which He received from the sins of this parish. Unite yourselves with my prayers for the parish so that His sufferings may be bearable. Thank you for having responded to my call. Try to come in ever greater numbers."

March 29, 1984

"Dear children!

In a special way this evening I am calling you to perseverance in trials. Consider how the Almighty is still suffering today on account of your sins. So when sufferings come, offer them up as a sacrifice to God. Thank you for having responded to my call."

April 5, 1984

"Dear children!

This evening I ask you especially to venerate the Heart of my Son, Jesus. Make reparation for the wound inflicted on the Heart of my Son. That Heart is offended by all kinds of sins. Thank you for coming this evening."

April 12, 1984

"Dear children!

Today I beseech you to stop slandering and to pray for the unity of the parish, because I and my Son have a special plan for this parish. Thank you for having responded to my call."

April 19, 9184 (Holy Thursday)

"Dear children!

Sympathize with me! Pray, pray, pray!"

April 30, 1984

Marija asked Our Lady, "Dear Madonna, why didn't you give me a message for the parish on Thursday?" Our Lady replied, "I do not wish to force anyone to do that which he/she neither feels nor desires, even though I had special messages for the parish by which I wanted to awaken the faith of every believer. But only a really small number has accepted my Thursday messages. In the beginning there were quite a few. But it's become a routine affair from them. And now recently some are asking for the message out of curiosity, and not out of faith and devotion to my Son and me."

May 10, 1984

Many of the faithful felt shaken by the last message of Our Lady. SOme had the feeling that Our Lady would not give any more messages to the parish, but this evening she said, "I am speaking to you and I wish to speak further. You just listen to my instructions!"

May 17, 1984

"Dear children!

Today I am very happy because there are many who want to consecrate themselves to me. Thank you. You have not made a mistake. My Son, Jesus Christ, wishes to bestow on you special graces through me. My Son is happy because of your dedication. Thank you for having responded to my call."

May 24, 1984

"Dear children!

I have told you already that I have chosen you in a special way, just the way you are. I, the Mother, love you all. And in any moment that is difficult for you, do not be afraid! Because I love you even then when you are far from me and my Son. Please, do not let my heart weep with tears of blood because of the souls who are lost in sin. Therefore, dear children, pray, pray, pray! Thank you for having responded to my call."

May 31, 1984

There were many people present from abroad. Our Lady did not give a message for the parish. She told Marija that she would give a message on Saturday to be announced at the Sunday parish Mass.

June 2, 1984 (Saturday)

"Dear children!

Tonight I wish to tell you during the days of this novena to pray for the outpouring of the Holy Spirit on your families and on your parish. Pray, and you shall not regret it. God will give you gifts by which you will glorify Him till the end of your life on this earth. Thank you for having responded to my call."

June 9, 1984 (Saturday)

"Dear children!

Tomorrow night pray for the Spirit of Truth! Especially, you from the parish. Because you need the Spirit of Truth to be able to convey the messages just the way they are, neither adding anything to them, nor taking anything whatsoever away from them, but just the way I said them. Pray for the Holy Spirit to inspire you with the spirit of prayer, so you will pray more. I, your Mother, tell you that you are praying little. Thank you for having responded to my call."

June 21, 1984

Pray, pray, pray! Thank you for having responded to my call."

July 12, 1984

"Dear children!

These days Satan wants to frustrate my plans. Pray that his plan not be realized. I will pray my Son Jesus to give you the grace to experience the victory of Jesus in the temptations of Satan. Thank you for having responded to my call."

July 19, 1984

"Dear children!

These days you have been experiencing how Satan is working. I am always with you, and don't you be afraid of temptations because God is always watching over us. Also, I have given myself to you and I sympathize with you even in the smallest temptation. Thank you for having responded to my call."

July 26, 1984

"Dear children!

Today also I wish to call you to persistent prayer and penance. Especially, let the young people of this parish be more active in their prayers. Thank you for having responded to my call."

August 2, 1984

"Dear children!

Today I am joyful and I thank you for your prayers. Pray still more these days for the conversion of sinners. Thank you for having responded to my call."

August 11, 1984 (Saturday)

"Dear children!

Pray, because Satan wishes to complicate my plans still further. Pray with the heart and surrender yourselves to Jesus in prayer."

August 14, 1984 (Tuesday)

This apparition was unexpected. Ivan was praying at home. After that he started to get ready to go to Church for the evening services. By surprise Our Lady appeared to him and told him to relate to the people, "I would like the people to pray along with me these days. And to pray as much as possible! And to fast strictly on Wednesdays and Fridays, and every day to pray at least one Rosary; the joyful, sorrowful and glorious mysteries." Our Lady asked that we accept this message with a firm will. She especially requested this of the parishioner and the faithful of the surrounding places.

August 16, 1984

"Dear children!

I beseech you, especially those from this parish, to live my messages and convey them to others, to whomever you meet. Thank you for having responded to my call."

August 23, 1984

"Dear children!

Pray, pray!" Marija said that she also invited the people, and especially the young people, to keep order during the Mass.

August 30, 1984

"Dear children!

The cross was also in God's plan when you built it. These days, especially, go on the mountain and pray before the cross. I need your prayers. Thank you for having responded to my call."

September 6, 1984

"Dear children!

Without prayer there is no peace. Therefore I say to you, dear children, pray at the foot of the cross for peace. Thank you for having responded to my call."

September 13, 1984

"Dear children!

I still need your prayers. You wonder why all these prayers? Look around you, dear children, and you will see how greatly sin has dominated the world. Pray, therefore, that Jesus conquers. Thank you for having responded to my call."

September 20, 1984

"Dear children!

Today I call on you to begin fasting with the heart. There are many people who are fasting, but only because everyone else is fasting. It has become a custom which no one wants to stop. I ask the parish to fast out of gratitude because God has allowed me to stay this long in this parish. Dear children, fast and pray with the heart. Thank you for having responded to my call."

September 27, 1984

"Dear children!

You have helped me along by your prayers to realize my plans. Keep on praying that my plans may be completed. I request the families of the parish to pray the family rosary. Thank you for having responded to my call."

October 4, 1984

"Dear children!

Today I want to tell you that again and again you make me happy by your prayer, but there are enough of those in this very parish who do not pray and my heart is saddened. Therefore pray that I can bring all your sacrifices and prayers to the Lord. Thank you for having responded to my call."

October 8, 1984 (Monday)

(Jakov was sick and received this message at home.)

"Dear children, let all the prayers you say in your homes in the evening be for the conversion of sinner because the world is in great sin. Every evening pray the rosary."

October 11, 1984

"Dear children!

Thank you for dedicating all your hard work to God even now when He is testing you through the grapes you are picking. Be assured, dear children, that He loves you and, therefore, He tests you. you just always offer up all your burdens to God and do not be anxious. thank you for having responded to my call."

October 18, 1984

"Dear children!

Today I call on you to read the bible every day in your homes and let it be in a visible place so as always to encourage you to read it and to pray. Thank you for having responded to my call."

October 25, 1984

"Dear children!

Pray during this month. God allows me every day to help you with graces to defend yourselves against evil. This is my month. I want to give it to you. you just pray and God will give you the graces you are seeking. I will help along with it. Thank you for having responded to my call."

November 1, 1984

"Dear children!

Today I call you to the renewal of prayer in your homes. The work in the fields is over. Now devote yourselves to prayer. Let prayer take the first place in your families. Thank you for having responded to my call."

November 8, 1984

"Dear children!

You are not conscious of the messages which God is sending you through me. His giving you great graces and you do not comprehend them. Pray to the Holy Spirit for enlightenment. If you only knew how great are the graces God is granting you, you would be praying without ceasing. Thank you for having responded to my call."

November 15, 1984

"Dear children!

You are a chosen people and God has given you great graces. You are not conscious of every message which I am giving you. Now I just want to say—pray, pray, pray! I don't know what else to tell you because I love you and I want you to comprehend my love and God's love through prayer. Thank you for having responded to my call."

November 22, 1984

"Dear children!

These days live all the main messages and keep rooting them in your hearts till Thursday. Thank you for having responded to my call."

November 29, 1984

"Dear children!

No, you don't know how to love an you don't know how to listen with love to the words I am saying o you. Be conscious, my beloved, that I am your Mother and I have come on earth to teach you to listen out of love, to pray out of love and not compelled by the fact that you are carrying a cross. By means of the cross God is glorified through every person. Thank you for having responded to my call."

December 6, 1984

"Dear children!

These days, I am calling you to family prayer. In God's Name many times I have been giving you messages, but you have not listened to me. This Christmas will be unforgettable for you only if you accept the messages which I am giving you. Dear children don't allow that day of joy to become my most sorrowful day. Thank you for having responded to my call."

December 14, 1984

"Dear children!

You know that the season of joy is getting closer, but without love you will achieve nothing. So first of all, begin to love your own family, everyone in the parish, and then you'll be able to love and accept all who are coming over here. Now let these seven days be a week when you need to learn to love. Thank you for having responded to my call."

December 20, 1984

"Dear children!

Today I am inviting you to do something concrete for Jesus Christ. As a sign of dedication to Jesus I want each family of the parish to bring a single flower before that happy day. I want every member of the family to have a single flower by the crib so Jesus can come and see your dedication to Him! Thank you for having responded to my call."

December 21, 1984 (Friday)

I want you to be a flower which will blossom for jesus on Christmas. And a flower that will not stop blooming when Christmas is over, I want your hearts to be shepherds to Jesus." (Message given through Jelena Vasilj.)

December 28, 1984

"Dear children!

This Christmas Satan wanted in a special way to spoil God's plans. You, dear children, have discerned Satan even on Christmas day itself. But God is winning in all your hearts. So let your hearts keep on being happy. Thank you for having responded to my call."

January 3, 1985

"Dear children!

These days the Lord has bestowed upon you great graces. Let this week be one of thanksgiving for all the graces which God has granted you. Thank you for having responded to my call."

January 10, 1985

"Dear children!

Today I want to thank you for all you sacrifices, but special thanks to those who have become dear to my heart and come here gladly. There are enough parishioners who are not listening to the messages, but because of those who are in a special way close to my heart, because of them, I am giving messages for the parish. And I will go on giving them because I love you and I want you to spread my messages with your heart. Thank you for having responded to my call."

January 14, 1985 (Monday)

"My dear children!

Satan is so strong and with all his might wants to disturb my plans which I have begun with you. you pray, just pray and don't stop for a minute! I will pray to my Son for the realization of all the plans I have begun. Be patient and constant in your prayers. And don't let Satan discourage you. He is working hard in the world. be on your guard!" (Message conveyed by Vicka from Our Lady.)

January 17, 1985

"Dear children!

These days Satan is working underhandedly against this parish, and you, dear children, have fallen asleep in prayer, and only some are going to Mass. Withstand the days of temptation! Thank you for having responded to my call."

January 24, 1985

"Dear children!

These days you have experienced God's sweetness, through the renewals which have been in this parish. Satan wants to work still more fiercely to take away your joy from each one of you. By prayer you can completely disarm him and ensure your happiness. Thank you for having responded to my call."

January 31, 1985

"Dear children!

Today I wish to tell you to open your hearts to God like the spring flowers which crave for the sun. I am your Mother and I always want you to be closer to the Father and that He will always give abundant gifts to your hearts. Thank you for having responded to my call."

February 7, 1985

"Dear children!

These days Satan is manifesting himself in a special way in this parish. Pray, dear children, that God's plan is brought into effect and that every work of Satan ends up for the glory of God. I have stayed with you this long so I might help you along in your trials. Thank you for having responded to my call."

February 14, 1985

"Dear children!

Today is the day when I give you a message for the parish, but the whole parish is not accepting the messages and is not living them. I am saddened and I want you, dear children, to listen to me and to live my messages. Every family must pray family prayer and read the Bible! Thank you for having responded to my call."

February 21, 1985

"Dear children!

From day to day I have been inviting you to renewal and prayer in the parish, but you are not accepting it. Today I am calling you for the last time! Now it's Lent and you as a parish can turn to my messages during Lent out of love. If you do not do that, I do not wish to keep on giving messages. God is permitting me that. Thank you for having responded to my call."

February 28, 1985

"Dear children!

Today I call you to live the word this week. 'I love God!' Dear children through love you will achieve everything and even what you think is impossible. God wants this parish to belong completely to Him. And that' what I want too. Thank you for having responded to my call."

March 7, 1985
"Dear children!

Today I call you to renew prayer in your families. Dear children, encourage the very young to prayer and the children to go to Holy Mass. Thank you for having responded to my call."

March 14, 1985
"Dear children!

In your life you have all experienced light and darkness. God grants to every person to recognize good and evil. I am calling you to the light which you should carry to all the people who are in darkness. People who are in darkness daily come into your homes. Dear children, give them the light! Thank you for having responded to my call."

March 21, 1985

"Dear children!

I wish to keep on giving messages and therefore today I call you to live and accept my messages! Dear children, I love you and in a special way I have chosen this parish, one more dear to me than the others, in which I have gladly remained when the Almighty sent me. Therefore I call on you—accept me, dear children, that it might go well with you. Listen to my messages! Thank you for having responded to my call."

March 24, 1985 (Sunday)

"Today I wish to call you all to confession, even if you have confessed a few days ago. I wish that you all experience my feast day within yourselves. But you cannot experience it unless you abandon yourselves completely to God. Therefore, I am inviting you all to reconciliation with God!"

March 28, 1985

"Dear children!

Today I wish to call you to pray, pray, pray! In prayer you shall perceive the greatest joy and the way out of every situation that has no exit. Thank you for starting up prayer. Each individual is dear to my heart. And I thank all who have urged prayer in their families. Thank you for having responded to my call."

April 4, 1985 (Holy Thursday)

"Dear children!

I thank you for having started to think more about God's glory in your hearts. Today is the day when I wished to stop giving the messages because some individuals did not accept me. The parish has been moved and I wish to keep giving you messages as it has never been done in history, from the beginning of the world. Thank you for having responded to my call."

April 5, 1985

"You parishioners have a great and heavy cross, but don't be afraid to carry it. My Son is here who will help you." (Message given through Ivanka.)

April 11, 1985

"Dear children!

Today I wish to say to everyone in the parish to pray in a special way to the Holy Spirit for enlightenment. From today God wishes me to test the parish in a special way in order that He might strengthen it in faith. Thank you for having responded to my call."

April 18, 1985

"Dear children!

Today I thank you for every opening of your hearts. Joy overtakes me for every heart that is opened to God especially from the parish. Rejoice with me! Pray all the prayers fro the opening of sinful hearts. I desire that God desires that through me. Thank you for having responded to my call."

April 25, 1985

"Dear children!

Today I wish to tell you to begin to work in your hearts as you are working in the fields. Work and change your hearts so that a new spirit from God can take its place in your hearts. Thank you for having responded to my call."

May 2, 1985

"Dear children!

Today I call you to prayer with the heart and not just from habit. Some are coming, but do not wish to move ahead in prayer. Therefore, I wish to warn you like a Mother: pray that prayer prevails in your hearts in every moment. Thank you for having responded to my call."

May 9, 1985

"Dear children!

No, you do not know how many graces God is giving you. you do not want to move ahead during these days when the Holy Spirit is working in a special way. Your hearts are turned toward the things of earth and they preoccupy you. Turn your hearts toward prayer and seek the Holy Spirit to be poured out on you. Thank you for having responded to my call."

May 16, 1985

"Dear children!

I am calling you to a more active prayer and attendance at Holy Mass. I wish your Mass to be an experience of God. I wish especially to say to the young people: be open to the Holy Spirit because God wishes to draw you to Himself in these days when Satan is at work. Thank you for having responded to my call."

May 23, 1985

"Dear children!

These days I call you especially to open your hearts to the Holy Spirit. Especially during these days the Holy Spirit is working through you. Open your hearts and surrender your life to Jesus so that He works through your hearts and strengthens you in faith. Thank you for having responded to my call."

May 30, 1985

"Dear children!

I call you again to prayer with the heart. Let prayer, dear children, be your every day food in a special way when your work in the fields is so wearing you out that you cannot pray with the heart. Pray, and then you shall overcome even every weariness. Prayer will be your joy and your rest. Thank you for having responded to my call."

June 6, 1985

"Dear children!

During these days people from all nations will be coming into the parish. And now I am calling you to love: love first of all your own household members, and then you will be able to accept and love all who are coming. Thank you for having responded to my call."

June 13, 1985

"Dear children!

Until the anniversary day I am calling you, the parish, to pray more and to let your prayer be a sign of surrender to God. Dear children, I know that you are all tired, but you don't know how to surrender yourselves to me. During these days surrender yourselves completely to me! Thank you for having responded to my call."

June 20, 1985

"Dear children!

For this Feast Day I wish to tell you to open your hearts to the Master of all hearts. Give me all your feelings and all your problems! I wish to comfort you in all your trials. I wish to fill you with peace, joy and love of God. Thank you for having responded to my call."

June 25, 1985

"I invite you to call on everyone to pray the Rosary. With the rosary you shall overcome all the adversities which Satan is trying to inflict on the Catholic Church. All you priests pray the Rosary! Dedicate your time to the Rosary!" (This message Our Lady gave in response to the question of Marija Pavlovic: "Our Lady, what do you wish to recommend to priests?")

June 28, 985

"Dear children!

Today I am giving you a message through which I desire to call you to humility. These days you have felt great joy because of all the people who have come and to whom you could tell your experiences with love. Now I invite you to continue in humility and with an open heart speak to all who are coming. Thank you for having responded to my message."

July 4, 1985

"Dear children!

I thank you for every sacrifice you have offered. And now I urge you to offer every sacrifice with love. I wish you, the helpless ones, to begin helping with confidence and the Lord will keep on giving to you in confidence. Thank you for having responded to my call."

July 11, 1985

"Dear children!

I love the parish and with my mantle I protect it from every work of Satan. Pray that Satan retreats from the parish and from every individual who comes into the parish. In that way you shall be able to hear every call of God and answer it with your life. Thank you for having responded to my call."

July 18, 1985

"Dear children!

Today I call you to place more blessed objects in your homes and that everyone put some blessed objects on the their person. bless all the objects and thus Satan will attack you less because you will have armor against him. Thank you for having responded to my call."

July 25, 1985

"Dear children!

I desire to lead you, but you do not wish to listen to my messages. Today I am calling you to listen to the messages and then you will be able to live everything which God tells me to convey to you. Open yourselves to God and God will work through you and keep on giving you everything you need. Thank you for having responded to my call."

August 1, 1985

"Dear children!

I wish to tell you that I have chosen this parish and that I am guarding it in my hands like a little flower that does not want to die. I call you to surrender to me so that I can keep on presenting you to God, fresh and without sin. Satan has taken part of the plan and wants to possess it. Pray that he does not succeed in that, because I wish you for myself so I can keep on giving you to God. Thank you for having responded to my call."

August 8, 1985

"Dear children!

Today I call you especially now to advance against Satan by means of prayer. Satan wants to work still more now that you know he is at work. Dear children, put on the armor for battle and with the Rosary in you hand defeat him! Thank you for having responded to my call."

August 15, 1985

"Dear children!

Today I am blessing you and I wish to tell you that I love you and that I urge you to live my messages. Today I am blessing you with the solemn blessing that the Almighty grants me. Thank you for having responded to my call."

August 22, 1985

"Dear children!

Today I wish to tell you that God wants to send you trials which you can overcome by prayer. God is testing you through daily chores. Now pray to peacefully withstand every trial. From everything through which God tests you come out more open to God and approach Him with love. Thank you for having responded to my call."

August 29, 1985

"Dear children!

I am calling you to prayer! Especially since Satan wishes to take advantage of the yield of your vineyards. Pray that Satan does not succeed in his plan. Thank you for having responded to my call."

September 5, 1985

"Dear children!

Today I thank you for all the prayers. Keep on praying all the more so that satan will be far away from this place. Dear children, Satan's plan has failed. Pray for fulfillment of what God plans in this parish. I especially thank the young people of the sacrifices they have offered up. Thank you for having responded to my call."

September 12, 1985

"Dear children!

I wish to tell you that the cross should be central these days. Pray especially before the cross from which great graces are coming. Now in your homes make a special consecration to the cross. Promise that you will neither offend Jesus nor abuse the cross. Thank you for having responded to my call."

September 20, 1985 (Friday)

"Dear children!

Today I invite you to live in humility all the messages which I am giving you. Do not become arrogant living the messages and saying, 'I am living the messages.' If you shall bear and live the messages in your heart, everyone will feel it so that words, which serve those who do not obey, will not be necessary. For you, dear children, it is necessary to live and witness by your lives. Thank you for having responded to my call."

September 26, 1985

"Dear children!

I thank you for all the prayers. Thank you for all the sacrifices. I wish to tell you, dear children, to renew the messages which I am giving you. Especially live the fast, because by fasting you will achieve and cause me the joy of the whole plan, which God is planning here in Medjugorje, being fulfilled. Thank you for having responded to my call."

October 3, 1985

"Dear children!

I wish to tell you to thank God for all the graces which God has given you. For all the fruits thank the Lord and glorify Him! Dear children, learn to give thanks in little things and then you will be able to give thanks also for the big things. Thank you for having responded to my call."

October 10, 1985

"Dear children!

I wish also today to call you to live the messages in the parish. Especially I wish to call the youth of the parish, who are dear to me. Dear children, if you live the messages, you are living the seed of holiness. I, as the Mother, wish to call you all to holiness so that you can bestow it on others. You are a mirror to others! Thank you for having responded to my call."

October 17, 1985

"Dear children!

Everything has its own time. Today I call you to start working on your own hearts. Now that all the work in the field is over, you are finding time for cleaning even the most neglected areas, but you leave your heart aside. Work more and clean with love every part of your heart. Thank you for having responded to my call."

October 24, 1985

"Dear children!

From day to day I wish to clothe you in holiness, goodness, obedience and God's love, so that from day to day you become more beautiful and more prepared for your Master. Dear children, listen to and live my messages. I wish to guide you. Thank you for having responded to my call."

October 31, 1985

"Dear children!

Today I wish to call you to work in the Church. I love all the same and I desire from each one to work as much as possible. I know , dear children, that you can, but you do not wish to because you feel small and humble, in these things. You need to be courageous and with little flowers do your share for the church and for Jesus so that everyone can be satisfied. Thank you for having responded to my call."

November 7, 1985

"Dear children!

I am calling you to the love of neighbor and love toward the one from whom evil comes to you. In that way with love you will be able to discern the intentions of hearts. Pray and love, dear children! By love you are able to do even that which you think is impossible. Thank you for having responded to my call."

November 14, 1985

"Dear children!

I, your Mother, love you and wish to urge you to prayer. I am tireless, dear children, and I am calling you even then, when you are far away from my heart. I am a Mother, and even though I feel pain for each one who goes astray, I forgive easily and am happy for every child who returns to me. Thank you for having responded to my call."

November 21, 1985

"Dear children!

I want to tell you that this season is especially for you from the parish. When it is summer, you saw that you have a lot of work. Now you don't have work in the fields, work on your own self personally! Come to Mass because this is the season given to you. Dear children, there are enough of those who come regularly despite bad weather because they love me and wish to show their love in a special way. What I want from you is to show me your love by coming to Mass, and the Lord will reward you abundantly. Thank you for having responded to my call."

November 28, 1985

"Dear children!

I want to thank everyone for all you have done for me, especially the youth. I beseech you, dear children, come to prayer with awareness. In prayer you shall come to know the greatness of God. Thank you for having responded to my call."

December 5, 1985

"Dear children!

I am calling you to prepare yourselves for Christmas by means of penance, prayer and works of charity. Dear children, do not look toward material things, because then you will not be able to experience Christmas. Thank you for having responded to my call."

December 12, 1985

"Dear children!

For Christmas my invitation is that together we glorify Jesus. I present Him to you in a special way on that day and my invitation to you is that on that day we glorify Jesus and His nativity. Dear children, on that day pray still more and think more about Jesus. Thank you for having responded to my call."

December 19, 1985

"Dear children!

Today I wish to call you to love of neighbor. The more you will to love your neighbor, the more you shall experience Jesus especially on Christmas Day. God will bestow great gifts on you if you surrender yourselves to Him. I wish in a special way on Christmas Day to give mothers my own special motherly blessing, and Jesus will bless the rest with His own blessing. Thank you for having responded to my call."

December 26, 1985

"Dear children!

I wish to thank all who have listened to my messages and who on Christmas Day have lived what I said. Undefiled by sin from now on, I wish to lead you further in love. Abandon your hearts to me! Thank you for having responded to my call."

January 2, 1986

"Dear children!

I call you to decide completely for God. I beseech you, dear children, to surrender yourselves completely and you shall be able to live everything I am telling you. It shall not be difficult for you to surrender yourselves completely to God. Thank you for having responded to my call."

January 9, 1986

"Dear children!

I call you by your prayers to help Jesus along in the fulfillment of all the plans which He is forming here. And offer your sacrifices to Jesus in order that everything is fulfilled the way He has planned it and that Satan can accomplish nothing. Thank you for having responded to my call."

January 16, 1986

"Dear children!

Today also I am calling you to prayer. Your prayers are necessary to me so that God may be glorified through all of you. Dear children, I pray you, obey and live the Mother's invitation, because only out of love am I calling you in order that I might help you. Thank you for having responded to my call."

January 23, 1986

"Dear children!

Again I call you to prayer with the heart. If you pray with the heart, dear children, the ice of your bothers will melt and every barrier shall disappear. Conversion will be easy for all who desire to accept it. That is the gift which by prayer you must obtain for your neighbor. Thank you for having responded to my call."

January 30, 1986

"Dear children!

Today I call you all to pray that God's plans for us may be realized and also everything that God desires through you! Help others to be converted, especially those who are coming to Medjugorje. Dear children, do not allow Satan to get control of your hearts, so you would be an image of Satan and not of me. I call you to pray for how you might be witness of my presence. Without you, God cannot bring to reality that which He desires. God has given a free will to everyone, and it's in your control. Thank you for having responded to my call."

February 6, 1986

"Dear children!

This parish, which I have chosen, is special and different from others. And I am giving great graces to all who pray with the heart. Dear children, I am giving the messages first of all to the residents of the parish, and then to all the others. First of all you must accept the messages, and then the others. You shall be answerable to me and my Son, Jesus. Thank you for having responded to my call."

February 13, 1986

"Dear children!

This Lent is a special incentive for you to change. Start from this moment. Turn off the television and renounce various things that are of no value. Dear children, I am calling you individually to conversion. This season is for you. Thank you for having responded to my call."

February 20, 1986

"Dear children!

The second message of these Lenten days is that you renew prayer before the cross. Dear children, I am giving you special graces and Jesus is giving you special gifts form the cross. Take them and live! Reflect on Jesus' Passion and in your life be united with Jesus! Thank you for having responded to my call."

February 27, 1986

"Dear children!

In humility live the messages which I am giving you. Thank you for having responded to my call."

March 6, 1986

"Dear children!

Today I call you to open yourselves more to God, so that He can work through you. The more you open yourselves, the more you receive the fruits. I wish to call you again to prayer. Thank you for having responded to my call."

March 13, 1986

"Dear children!

Today, I call you to live Lent by means of your little sacrifices. Thank you for every sacrifice you have brought me. Dear children, live that way continuously, and with your love help me to present the sacrifice. God will reward you for that. Thank you for having responded to my call."

March 20, 1986

"Dear children!

Today I call you to approach prayer actively. You wish to live everything I am telling you, but you are not succeeding because you are not praying. Dear children, I beseech you to open yourselves and begin to pray. Prayer will be your joy. If you make a start it won't be boring to you because you will be praying out of joy. Thank you for having responded to my call."

March 27, 1986

"Dear children!

I wish to thank you for all the sacrifices and I invite you to the greatest sacrifice, the sacrifice of love. Without love, you are not able to accept either me or my Son. Without love, you cannot give an account of your experiences to others. Therefore, dear children, I call you to begin to live love within yourselves. Thank you for having responded to my call."

April 3, 1986

"Dear children!

I wish to call you to a living of the Holy Mass. There are many of you who have sensed the beauty of the Holy mass, but there are also those who come unwillingly. I have chosen you, dear children, but Jesus gives you His graces in the mass. Therefore, consciously live the Holy Mass and let your coming to it be a joyful one. Come to it with love and make the mass your own. Thank you for having responded to my call."

April 10, 1986

"Dear children!

I desire to call you to grow in love. A flower is not able to grow normally without water. So also you, dear children, are not able to grow without God's blessing. From day to day you need to seek His blessing so you will grow normally and perform all your actions in union with God. Thank you for having responded to my call."

April 17, 1986

"Dear children!

You are absorbed with material things, but in the material you lose everything that God wishes to give you. I call you, dear children, to pray for the gifts of the Holy Spirit which are necessary for you now in order to be able to give witness to my presence here and to all that I am giving you. Dear children, let go to me so I can lead you completely. Don't be absorbed with material things. Thank you for having responded to my call."

April 24, 1986

"Dear children!

Today my invitation is that you pray. Dear children, you are forgetting that you are all important. The elderly are especially important to the family. urge them to pray. Let all the young people be an example to others by their life and let them witness to Jesus. Dear children, I beseech you, begin to change through prayer and you will know what you need to do. Thank you for having responded to my call."

May 1, 1986

"Dear children!

I beseech you to start changing your life in the family. Let the family be a harmonious flower that I wish to give to Jesus. Dear children, let every family be active in prayer for I wish that the fruits in the family be seen one day. Only that way shall I give you all, like petals, as a gift to Jesus in fulfillment of God's plans. Thank you for having responded to my call."

May 8, 1986

"Dear children!

You are the ones responsible for the messages. The source of grace is here, but you, dear children, are the vessels which transport the gifts. Therefore, dear children, I am calling you to do your job with responsibility. Each one shall be responsible according to his own ability. Dear children, I am calling you to give the gifts to others with love and not to keep them for yourselves. Thank you for having responded to my call."

May 15, 1986

"Dear children!

Today I call you to give me your heart so I can change it to be like mine. You are wondering, dear children, why you cannot respond to that which I am seeking from you. You are not able to because you have not given me your heart so I can change it. you are talking but you are not doing. I call on you to do everything that I am telling you. That way I will be with you. Thank you for having responded to my call."

May 22, 1986

"Dear children!

Today I wish to give you my own love. You do not know, dear children, how great my love is, and you do not know ho to accept it. In various ways I wish to show it to you but you, dear children, do not recognize it. You do not understand my words with your heart and neither are you able to comprehend my love. Dear children, accept me in your life and so you will be able to accept all I am saying to you and to which I am calling you. Thank you for having responded to my call."

May 29, 1986

"Dear children!

Today my call to you is that in your life you live love toward God and neighbor. Without love, dear children, you can do nothing. Therefore, dear children, I am calling you to live in mutual love. Only in that way will be able to love and accept both me and all those around you who are coming into the parish. everyone will sense my love through you. Therefore, I beseech you, dear children, to start loving from today with an ardent love, the love with which I love you. Thank you for having responded to my call."

June 5, 1986

"Dear children!

Today I am calling on you to decide whether or not you wish to live the messages which I am giving you. I wish you to be active in living and spreading the messages. Especially, dear children, I wish that you all be the reflection of Jesus, which will enlighten this unfaithful world walking in darkness. I wish all of you to be the light for everyone and that you give witness in the light. Dear children, you are not called to the darkness, but you are called to the light. Therefore, live the light with your own life. Thank you for having responded to my call."

June 12, 1986

"Dear children!

Today I call you to begin to pray the Rosary with a living faith. That way I will be able to help you. You, dear children, wish to obtain graces, but you are not praying, I am not able to help you because you do not want to get started. Dear children, I am calling you to pray the Rosary and that your Rosary be an obligation which you shall fulfill with joy. That way you shall understand the reason I am with you this long. I desire to teach you to pray. Thank you for having responded to my call."

June 19, 1986

"Dear children!

During these days my Lord is allowing me to be able to intercede more graces for you. Therefore, I wish to urge you once more to pray, dear children! Pray without ceasing! That way I will give you the joy which the Lord gives to me. With these graces, dear children. I want your sufferings to be a joy. I am you Mother and I desire to help you. Thank you for having responded to my call."

June 26, 1986

"Dear children!

God is allowing me along with Himself to bring about this oasis of peace. I wish to call on you to protect it and that the oasis always be unspoiled. There are those who by their carelessness are destroying the peace and the prayer. I am inviting you to give witness and by your own life to help to preserve the peace. Thank you for having responded to my call."

July 3, 1986

"Dear children!

Today I am calling you all to prayer. Without prayer, dear children, you are not able to experience either God, or me or the graces which I am giving you. Therefore, my call to you is that the beginning and end of your day always be prayer. Dear children, I wish to lead you daily more and more in prayer, but you are not able to grow because you do not desire it. my call, dear children, is that for you prayer be in the first place. Thank you for having responded to my call."

July 10, 1986

"Dear children!

Today I am calling you to holiness. Without holiness you cannot live. Therefore, with love overcome every sin and with love overcome all the difficulties which are coming to you. Dear children, I beseech you to live love within yourselves. Thank you for having responded to my call."

July 17, 1986

"Dear children!

Today I am calling you to reflect upon why I am with you this long. I am the Mediatrix between you and God. Therefore, dear children, I desire to call you to live always out of love all that which God desires of you. For that reason, dear children, in your own humility live all the messages which I am giving you. Thank you for having responded to my call."

July 24, 1986

"Dear children!

I rejoice because of all of you who are on the way of holiness and I beseech you, by your own testimony help those who do not know how to live in holiness. Therefore, dear children, let your family be a place where holiness is birthed. Help everyone to live in holiness, but especially your own family. Thank you for having responded to my call."

July 31, 1986

"Dear children!

Hatred gives birth to dissensions and does not regard anyone or anything. I call you always to bring harmony an peace. Especially, dear children, in the place where you live, act with love. Let your only instrument always be love. By love turn everything into good which Satan desires to destroy and possess. Only that way shall you be completely mine and I shall be able to help you. Thank you for having responded to my call."

August 7, 1986

"Dear children!

You know that I promised you an oasis of peace, but you don't know that beside an oasis stands the desert, where Satan is lurking and wanting to tempt each one of you. Dear children, only by prayer are you able to overcome every influence of Satan in your place. I am with you, but I cannot take away your freedom. Thank you for having responded to my call."

August 14, 1986

"Dear children!

My call to you is that your prayer be the joy of an encounter with the Lord. I am not able to guide you as long as you yourselves do not experience joy in prayer. From day to day I desire to lead you more and more in prayer, but I do not wish to force you. Thank you for having responded to my call."

August 21, 1986

"Dear children!

I thank you for the love which you are showing me. You know, dear children, that I love you immeasurably and daily I pray the Lord to help you to understand the love which I am showing you. Therefore, you, dear children, pray, pray, pray!"

August 28, 1986

"Dear children!

My call is that in everything you would be am image for others, especially in prayer and witnessing. Dear children, without you I am not able to help the world. I desire that you cooperate with me in everything, even in the smallest things. Therefore, dear children, help me by letting your prayer be from the heart and all of you surrendering completely to me. That way I shall be able to teach and lead you on this way which I have begun with you. Thank you for having responded to my call."

September 4 1986

"Dear children!

Today again I am calling you to prayer and fasting. You know, dear children, that with your help I am able to accomplish everything and force Satan not to be seducing to evil and to remove himself from this place. Dear children, Satan is lurking for each individual. Especially in everyday affairs he wants to spread confusion among each one of you. Therefore, dear children, my call to you is that your day would be only prayer and complete surrender to God. Thank you for having responded to my call."

September 11, 1986

"Dear children!

For these days while you are joyful celebrating the cross, I desire that your cross also would be a joy for you. Especially, dear children, pray that you may be able to accept sickness and suffering with love the way Jesus accepted them. Only that way shall I be able with joy to give out to you the graces and healings which Jesus is permitting me. Thank you for having responded to my call."

September 18, 1986

"Dear children!

Today again I thank you for all that you have accomplished for me in these days. especially dear children, I thank you in the name of Jesus for the sacrifices which you offered in this past week. Dear children, you are forgetting that I desire sacrifices from you so I can help you and drive Satan away from you. Therefore, I am calling you again to offer sacrifices with a special reverence toward God. Thank you for having responded to my call."

September 25, 1986

"Dear children!

By your own peace I am calling you to help others to see and begin to seek peace. you, dear children, are at peace and not able to comprehend lack of peace. Therefore, I am calling you, so that by your prayer and your life you help to destroy everything that is evil in people and uncover the deception that Satan makes use of. You pray that the truth prevails in all hearts. Thank you for having responded to my call."

October 2, 1986

"Dear children!

Today again I am calling you to pray. you, dear children, are not able to understand how great the value of prayer is as long as you yourselves do not say: 'Now is the time for prayer, now nothing else is important to me, now not one person is important to me but God.' Dear children, consecrate yourselves to prayer with a special love so that God will be able to render graces back to you. Thank you for having responded to my call."

October 9, 1986

"Dear children!

You know that I desire to lead you on he way of holiness, but I do not want to compel you to be saints by force. I desire that each of you by your own little self-denials help yourself and me so I can lead you from day to day closer to holiness. Therefore, dear children, I do not desire to force you to observe the messages. but rather this long time that I am with you is a sign that I love you immeasurably and what I desire of each individual is to become holy. Thank you for having responded to my call."

October 16, 1986

"Dear children!

Today again I want to show you how much I love you, but I am sorry that I am not able to help each one to understand my love. Therefore, dear children, I am calling you to prayer and complete surrender to God, because Satan wants to sift you through everyday affairs and in your life he wants to snatch the first place. Therefore, dear children, pray without ceasing! Thank you for having responded to my call."

October 23, 1986

"Dear children!

Today again I am calling you to pray. Especially, dear children, do I call you to pray for peace. Without your prayers, dear children, I cannot help you to fulfill the message which the Lord has given me to give to you. Therefore, dear children, pray, so that in prayer you realize what God is giving you. Thank you for having responded to my call."

October 30, 1986

"Dear children!

Today again I desire to call you to take seriously and carry out the messages which I am giving you. Dear children, it is for your sake that I have stayed this long so I could help you to fulfill all the messages which I am giving you. Therefore, dear children, out of love for me carry out all the messages which I am giving you. Thank you for having responded to my call."

November 6, 1986

"Dear children!

Today I wish to call you to pray daily for souls in purgatory. For every soul prayer and grace is necessary to reach God and the love of God. By doing this, dear children, you obtain new intercessors who will help you in life to realize that all the earthly things are not important for you, that only Heaven is that for which it is necessary to strive. Therefore, dear children, pray without ceasing that you may be able to help yourselves and the others to whom your prayers bring joy. Thank you for having responded to my call."

November 13, 1986

"Dear children!

Today again I am calling you to pray with your whole heart and day by day to change your life. Especially, dear children, I am calling that by your prayers and sacrifices you begin to live in holiness, because I desire that each one of you who has been to this fountain of grace will come to Paradise with the special gift which you shall give me, and that is holiness. Therefore, dear children, pray and daily change your life in order to become fully holy. I shall always be close to you. Thank you for having responded to my call."

November 20, 1986

"Dear children!

Today also I am calling you to live and follow with a special love all the messages which I am giving you. Dear children, God does not want you lukewarm and undecided, but that you totally surrender to Him. You know that I love you and that out of love I long for you. Therefore, dear children, you also decide for love so that you will long for and daily experience God's love. Dear children, decide for love so that love prevails in all of you, but not human love, rather God's love. Thank you for having responded to my call."

November 7, 1986

"Dear children!

Again today I call you to consecrate your life to me with love, so I am able to guide you with love. I love you, dear children, with a special love and I desire to bring you all to Heaven unto God. I want you to realize that this life lasts briefly compared to the one in Heaven. Therefore, dear children, decide again today for God. Only that way will I be able to show how much you are dear to me and how much I desire all to be saved and to be with me in Heaven. Thank you for having responded to my call."

December 4, 1986

"Dear children!

Today, I call you to prepare your hearts of these days when the Lord particularly desires to purify you from all the sins of your past. You, dear children, are not able by yourselves, therefore I am here to help you. you pray, dear children! Only that way shall you be able to recognize all the evil that is in you and surrender it to the Lord so the Lord may completely purify your hearts. Therefore, dear children, pray without ceasing and prepare your hearts in penance and fasting. Thank you for having responded to my call."

December 11, 1986

"Dear children!

I am calling you to pray especially at this time in order to experience the joy of meeting with the newborn Jesus. Dear children, I desire that you experience these days just as I experienced them. With you I wish to guide you and show you the joy into which I desire to bring each one of you. Therefore, dear children, pray and surrender completely to me. Thank you for having responded to my call."

December 18, 1986

"Dear children!

Once again I desire to call you to prayer. When you pray you are much more beautiful, like flowers, which after the snow, show all their beauty and all their colors become indescribable. So also you, dear children, after prayer show before God all so much more what is beautiful and are beloved by Him. Therefore, dear children, pray and open your inner self to the Lord so that He makes of you a harmonious and beautiful flower for Paradise. Thank you for having responded to my call."

December 25, 1986 (Christmas Day)

"Dear children!

Today also I give thanks to the Lord for all that He is doing for me, especially for this gift that I am able to be with you also today. Dear children, these are the days in which the Father grants me special graces to all who open their hearts. I bless you and I desire that you too, dear children, become alive to the graces and place everything at God's disposal so that He may be glorified through you. My heart carefully follows your progress. Thank you for having responded to my call."

January 1, 1987

"Dear children!

Today I wish to call on all of you that in the new Year you live the messages which I am giving you. Dear children, you know that for your sake I have remained a long time so I might teach you how to make progress on the way of holiness. Therefore, dear children, pray without ceasing and live the messages which I am giving you for I am doing it with great love toward God and toward you. Than you for having responded to my call."

January 8, 1987

"Dear children!

I desire to thank you for every response to the messages. Especially, dear children, thank you for all the sacrifices and prayers which you have presented to me. Dear children, I desire to keep on giving you still further messages, only not every Thursday, dear children, but on each 25th in the month. The time has come when what my Lord desired has been fulfilled. Now I will give you less messages, but I am still with you. Therefore, dear children, I beseech you, listen to my messages and live the, so I can guide you. Dear children, thank you for having responded to my call."

January 25, 1987

"Dear children!

Behold, also today I want to call you to start living anew life as of today. Dear children, I want you to comprehend that God has chosen each one of you, in order to use you in His great plan of the salvation of mankind. You are not able to comprehend how great your role is in God's design. Therefore, dear children, pray so that in prayer you may be able to comprehend what God's plan is in your regard. I am with you in order that you may be able to bring it about in all its fullness. Thank you for having responded to my call."

February 25, 1987

"Dear children!

Today I want to wrap you all in my mantle and lead you all along the way of conversion. Dear children, I beseech you, surrender to the Lord your entire past, all the evil that has accumulated in your hearts. I want each one of you to be happy, but in sin nobody can be happy. Therefore, dear children, pray, and in prayer you shall realize a new way of joy. Joy will manifest in your hearts and thus you shall be joyful witnesses of that which I and My Son want from each one of you,. I am blessing you. Thank you for having responded to my call."

March 25, 1987

"Dear children!

Today I am grateful to you for your presence in this place, where I am giving you special graces. I call each one of you to begin to live as of today that life which God wishes of you and to begin to perform good works of love and mercy. I do not want you, dear children, to live the message and be committing sin which is displeasing to me. therefore, dear children, I want each of you to live a new life without destroying all that God produces in you and is giving you. I give you my special blessing and I am remaining with you on your way of conversion. Thank you for having responded to my call."

April 25, 1987

"Dear children!

Today also I am calling you to prayer. You know, dear children, that God grants special graces in prayer. Therefore, seek and pray in order that you may be able to comprehend all that I am giving here. I call you, dear children to prayer with the heart. You know that without prayer you cannot comprehend all that God is planning through each one of you. Therefore, pray! I desire that through each one of you God's plan may be fulfilled, that all which God has planted in your heart may keep on growing. So pray that God's blessing may protect each of you from all the evil that is threatening you. I bless you, dear children. Thank you for having responded to my call."

May 25, 1987

"Dear children!

I am calling everyone of you to start living in God's love. Dear children, you are ready to commit sin, and to put yourselves sin the hand of Satan without reflecting. I call on each one of you to consciously decide for God and against Satan. I am your Mother and, therefore, I want to lead you all to perfect holiness. I want each one of you to be happy here on earth and to be with me in Heaven. That is, dear children, the purpose of my coming here and it's my desire. Thank you for having responded to my call."

June 25, 1987

"Dear children!

Today I thank you and I want to invite you all to God's peace. I want each one of you to experience in your hear that peace which God gives. I want to bless you all today. I am blessing you with God's blessing and I beseech you, dear children, to follow and to live my way. I love you, dear children, and so not even counting the number times, I go on calling you and I thank you for all that you are doing for my intentions. I beg you, help me to present you to God and to save you. Thank you for having responded to my call."

July 25, 1987

"Dear children!

I beseech you to take up the way of holiness beginning today. I love you and, therefore, I want you to be holy. I do not want Satan to block you on that way. Dear children, pray and accept all that God is offering you on a way which is bitter. But at the same time, God will reveal every sweetness to whomever begins to go on that way, and He will gladly answer every call of God. Do not attribute importance to petty things. Long for Heaven. Thank you for having responded to my call."

August 25, 1987

"Dear children!

Today also I am calling you all in order that each one of you decides to live my messages. God has permitted me also in this year, which the Church has dedicated to me, to be able to speak to you and to be able to spur you on to holiness. Dear children, seek from God the graces which He is giving you through me. I am ready to intercede with God for all that you seek so that your holiness may be complete. Therefore, dear children, do not forget to seek, because God has permitted me to obtain graces for you. Thank you for having responded to my call."

September 25, 1987

"Dear children!

Today also I want to call you all to prayer. Let prayer be your life. Dear children, dedicate your time only to Jesus and He will give you everything that you are seeking. He will reveal Himself to you in fullness. Dear children, Satan is strong and is waiting to test each one of you. Pray, and that way he will neither be able to injure you nor block you on the way of holiness. Dear children, through prayer grow all the more toward God from day to day. Thank you for having responded to my call."

October 25, 1987

"Dear children!

Today I want to call all of you to decide for Paradise. The way is difficult for those who have not decide for God. Dear children, decide and believe that God is offering Himself to you in His fullness. You are invited and you need to answer the call of the Father, Who is calling you through me. Pray, because is prayer each one of you will be able to achieve complete love. I am blessing you and I desire to help you so that each one of you might be under my motherly mantle. Thank you for having responded to my call."

November 25, 1987

"Dear children!

Today also I call each one of you to decide to surrender again everything completely to me. Only that way will I be able to present each of you to God. Dear children, you know that I love you immeasurably and that I desire each of you for myself, but God has given to all a freedom which I lovingly respect and humbly submit to, I desire, dear children, that yo help so that everything God has planned in this parish shall be realized. If you do not pray, you shall not be able to recognize my love, and the plans which God has for this parish and for each individual. Pray that Satan does not entice you with his pride and deceptive strength. i am with you and I want you to believe me, that I love you. Thank you for having responded to my call."

December 25, 1987

"Dear children!

Rejoice with me! My heart is rejoicing because of Jesus and today I wan to give Him to you. Dear children, I want each one of you to open your heart to Jesus and I will give Him to you with love. Dear children, I want Him to change you, to teach you and to protect you. Today I am praying in a special way for each one of you and I am presenting you to God so He will manifest Himself in you. I am calling you to sincere prayer with the heart so that every prayer of yours may be an encounter with God. In your work and in your everyday life, put God in the first place. I call you today with great seriousness to obey me and to do as I am calling you. Thank you for having responded to my call."

January 25, 1988

"Dear children!

Today again I am calling you to complete conversion, which is difficult for those who have not chosen God. God can give you everything that you seek from Him But you seek God only when sicknesses, problems and difficulties come to you and you think that God is far from you and is not listening and does not hear your prayers. No, dear children, that is not the truth. When you are far from God, you cannot receive graces because you do not seek them with a firm faith. Day by day, I am praying for you, and I want to draw you ever more near to God, but I cannot if you don't want it. Therefore, dear children, put your life in God's hands. I bless you all. Thank you for having responded to my call."

February 25, 1988

"Dear children!

Today again I am calling you to prayer to complete surrender to God. You know that I love you and am coming here out of love so I could show yo the path to peace and salvation for your souls. I want yo to obey me and not permit Satan to seduce you. Dear children, Satan is very strong and, therefore, I ask you to dedicate your prayers tome so that those who are under his influence can be saved. Give witness by your life. Sacrifice your lives for the salvation of the world. I am with you, and I am grateful to you, but in heaven you shall receive the Father's reward which he has promised to you. Therefore, dear children, do not be afraid. If you pray, Satan cannot injure you even a little bit because you are God's children and He is watching over you. Pray and let the rosary always be in your hand as a sign to Satan that you belong to me. Thank you for having responded to my call."

March 25, 1988

"Dear children!

Today also I am inviting you to a complete surrender to God. Dear children, you are not conscious of how God loves you with such a great love because He permits me to be with you so I can instruct you and help you to find the way of peace. This way, however, you cannot discover if you do not pray. Therefore, dear children, forsake everything and consecrate your time to God and God will bestow gifts upon you and bless you. Little children, don't forget that your life is fleeting like a spring flower which today is wondrously beautiful but tomorrow has vanished. Therefore, pray in such a way that your prayer, your surrender to God, may become like a road sign. That way, your witness will not only have value for yourselves but for all eternity. Thank you for having responded to my call."

April 25, 1988

"Dear children!

God wants to make you holy. Therefore, through me He is inviting you to complete surrender. Let holy Mass be your life. Understand that the church is God's palace, the place in which I gather you and want to show you the way to God. Come and pray. Neither look at others nor slander them, but rather, let your life be a testimony on the way of holiness. Churches deserve respect and are set apart as holy because God, who became man, dwells in them day and night. Therefore, little children, believe and pray that the Father increase your faith, and then ask for whatever you need. I am with you and I am rejoicing because of your conversion and I am protecting you with my motherly mantle. Thank you for having responded to my call."

May 25, 1988

"Dear children!

I am inviting you to a complete surrender to God. Pray, little children, that Satan may not carry you about like the branches in the wind. Be strong in God. I desire that through you the whole world may get to know the God of joy. By your life bear witness for God's joy. Do not be anxious nor worried. God himself will help you and show you the way. I desire that you love all men with my love. Only in that way can love reign over the world. Little children, you are mine. I love you and want you to surrender to me so that I can lead you to God. never cease praying so that Satan cannot take advantage of you. Pray for the knowledge that you are mine. I bless you with blessings of joy. Thank you for having responded to my call."

June 25, 1988

"Dear children!

I am calling you to that love which is loyal and pleasing to God. Little children, love bears everything bitter and difficult for the sake of Jesus who is love. Therefore, dear children, pray that God come to your aid, but according to His love. Surrender yourself to God so that He may hear you, console you and forgive everything inside you which is a hindrance on the way of love. In this way God can move your life, and you will grow in love. Dear children, glorify God with a hymn of love so that God's love may be able to grow in you day by day to its fullness. Thank you for having responded to my call."

July 25, 1988

"Dear children!

Today I am calling you to a complete surrender to God. Everything you do and everything you possess give over to God so that He can take control in your life as the King of all that you possess. That way, through me, God can lead you into the depths of the spiritual life. Little children, so not be afraid, because I am with you even if you think there is no way out and that Satan is in control. I am bringing peace to you. I am your Mother, the Queen of Peace. I am blessing you with the blessing of joy so that for you God may be everything in your life. Thank you for having responded to my call."

August25, 1988

"Dear children!

Today I invite you all to rejoice in the life which God gives you. Little children, rejoice in God, the Creator, because He has created you so wonderfully. Pray that your life be joyful thanksgiving which flows out of your heart like a river of joy. Little children, give thanks unceasingly for all that you possess, for each little gift which God has given you, so that a joyful blessing always comes down from God upon your life. Thank you for having responded to my call."

September 25, 1988

"Dear children!

Today I am inviting all of you, without exception, to the way of holiness in your life. God gave you the grace, the gift of holiness. Pray that you may, more and more, comprehend it, and in that way, you will be able, by your life, to bear witness for God. Dear children, I am blessing you and I intercede to God for you so that your way and your witness may be a complete one and a joy for God. Thank you for having responded to my call."

October 25, 1988

"Dear children!

My invitation that you live the messages which I am giving you is a daily one, especially, little children, because I want to draw you closer to the Heart of Jesus. Therefore, little children, I am inviting you today to the prayer of consecration to Jesus, my dear Son, so that each of you may be His. And then I am inviting you to the consecration of my Immaculate Heart. I want you to consecrate yourselves as parents, as families and as parishioners so that all belong to God through my heart. Therefore, little children, pray that you comprehend the greatness of this message which I am giving you. I do not want anything for myself, rather all for the salvation of your soul. Satan is strong and therefore, you, little children by constant prayer, press tightly against my motherly heart. Thank you for having responded to my call."

November 25, 1988

"Dear children!

I call you to prayer, to have an encounter with God in prayer. God gives Himself to you, but He wants you to answer in your own freedom to His invitation. That is why little children during they day, find yourselves a special time when you could pray in peace and humility, and have this meeting with god the Creator. I am with you and I intercede for you in front of God, so watch in vigil, so that every encounter in prayer be the joy of your contact with God. Thank you for having responded to my call."

December 25, 1988

"Dear children!

I call you to peace. Live it in your heart and all around you, so that all will know peace that does not come from you but from God. Little children, today is a great day. Rejoice with me. Glorify the Nativity of Jesus through the peace that I give you. It is for this peace that I have come as your Mother, Queen of Peace. Today I give you my special blessing. Bring it to all creation, so that all creation will know peace. Thank you for having responded to my call."

January 25, 1989

"Dear children!

Today I am calling you to the way of holiness. Pray that you amy comprehend the beauty and the greatness of this way where God reveals himself to you in a special way. Pray that you may be open to everything that God does through you that in your life you may be enabled to give thanks to God and to rejoice over everything that He does through each individual. I give you my blessing. Thank you for having responded to my call."

February 25, 1989

"Dear children!

Today I invite you to prayer of the heart. Throughout this season of grace I wish each of you to be united with Jesus, but without unceasing prayer you cannot experience the beauty and greatness of the grace which God is offering you. Therefore, little children, at all times, fill your heart with even the smallest prayers. I am with you and unceasingly keep watch over every heart which is given to me. Thank you for having responded to my call."

April 25, 1989

"Dear children!

I am calling you to a complete surrender to God. Let everything that you possess be in the hands of God. Only in that way shall you have joy in your heart. Little children, rejoice in everything that you have. Give thanks to God because everything is God's gift to you. That way in your life you shall be able to give thanks for everything and discover God in everything even in the smallest flower. Thank you for having responded to my call."

May 25, 1989

"Dear children!

I invite you now to be open to God. See, children, how nature is opening herself and is giving life and fruits. In the same way I invite you to live with God and to surrender completely to Him. Children, I am with you and I want to introduce you continually to the joy of life. I desire that everyone my discover the joy and love which only God can give. God doesn't want anything from you only your surrender. Therefore, children, decide seriously for God because God doesn't pass away. Pray to be able to discover the greatness and joy of life which God gives you. Thank you for having responded to my call."

June 25, 1989

"Dear children!

Today I am calling you to live the messages I have been giving you during the past eight years. This is the time of grace and I desire the grace of God be great for every single one of you. I am blessing you and I love you with a special love. Thank you for having responded to my call."

July 25, 1989

"Dear children!

Today I am calling you to renew your hearts. Open yourselves to God and surrender to Him all your difficulties and crosses, so God may turn everything into joy. Little children, you cannot open yourselves to God if you do not pray. Therefore, from today, decide to consecrate a time in the day only for an encounter with God in silence. In that way you will be able, with God, to witness my presence here. Little children, I do not wish to force you. Rather freely give God your time, like children of God. Thank you for having responded to my call."

August 25, 1989

"Dear children!

I call you to prayer. By means of prayer, little children, you obtain joy and peace. Through prayer you are richer in the mercy of God. Therefore, little children, let prayer be the life of each one of you. Especially I call you to pray so that all those who are far away from God may be converted. Then our hearts shall be richer because God will rule in the hearts of all men. Therefore, little children, pray, pray, pray! Let prayers begin to rule in the whole world. Thank you for having responded to my call."

September 25, 1989

"Dear children!

Today I invite you to give thanks to God for all the gifts you have discovered in the course of your life and even for the least gift that you have perceived. I give thanks with you and want all of you to experience the joy of these gifts. And I want God to be everything for each one of you. And then, little children, you can grow continuously on the way of holiness. Thank you for responding to my call."

October 25, 1989

"Dear children!

Today also I am inviting you to prayer. I am always inviting you, but you are still far away. Therefore, from today, decide seriously to dedicate time to God. I am with you and I wish to teach you to pray with the heart. In prayer with the heart you shall encounter God. Therefore, little children, pray, pray, pray! Thank you for having responded to my call."

November 25, 1989

"Dear children!

I am inviting you for years by these messages which I am giving you. Little children, by means of the messages I wish to make a very beautiful mosaic in your hearts, so I may be able to present each one of you to God like the original image. Therefore, little children, I desire that your decisions be free before God, because He has given you freedom. Therefore, pray, so that, free from any influence of Satan, we may decide only for God. I am praying for you before God and I am seeking your surrender to God. Thank you for having responded to my call."

December 25, 1989

"Dear children!

Today I bless you in a special way with my motherly blessing and I am interceding for you before God that He gives you the gift of conversion of the heart. For years I am calling you and exhorting you to a deep spiritual life in simplicity, but you are so cold. Therefore, little children, I ask you to accept and live the messages with seriousness, so that your soul will not be sad when I will no longer be with you like insecure children in their first steps. Therefore, little children, every day read the messages that i have given you and transform them into life. I love you and therefore I am calling you all to the way of salvation with God. Thank you for having responded to my call."

January 25, 1990

"Dear children!

Today I invite you to decide for God once again and to choose Him before everything and above everything, so that He may work miracles in your life and that day by day your life may become joy with Him. Therefore, little children, pray and do not permit Satan to work in your life through misunderstandings, the nonunderstanding and nonacceptance of one another. Pray that you may be able to comprehend the greatness and the beauty of the gift of life. Thank you for having responded to my call."

February 25, 1990

"Dear children!

I invite you to surrender to God. In this season I specially want you to renounce all the things to which you are attached but which are hurting your spiritual life. Therefore, little children, decide completely for God, and do not allow Satan to come into your life through those things that hurt both you and your spiritual life. Little children, God is offering Himself to you in fullness, and you can discover and recognize Him only in prayer. Therefore make a decision for prayer. Thank you for having responded to my call."

March 25, 1990

"Dear children!

I am with you even if yo are not conscious of it. I want to protect you from everything that Satan offers you and through which he wants to destroy you and through which he wants to destroy you. As I bore Jesus in my womb, so also, dear children, do I wish to bear you into holiness. God wants to save you and sends you messages through men, nature, and so many things which can only help you to understand that you must change the direction of your life. Therefore, little children, understand also the greatness of the gift which God is giving you through me, so that I may protect you with my mantle and lead you to the joy of life. Thank you for having responded to my call."

April 25, 1990

"Dear children!

Today I invite you to accept with seriousness and to live the messages which I am giving you. I am with you and I desire, dear children, that each one of you be ever closer to my heart. Therefore, little children, pray and seek the will of God in your everyday life. I desire that each one of you discover the way of holiness and grow in it until eternity. I will pray for you and intercede for you before God that you understand the greatness of this gift which God is giving me that I can be with you. Thank you for having responded to my call."

May 25, 1990

"Dear children!

I invite you to decide with seriousness to live this novena. Consecrate the time to prayer and to sacrifice. I am with you and I desire to help you to grow in renunciation and mortification, that you may be able to understand the beauty of the life of people who go on giving themselves to me in a special way. Dear children, God blesses you day after day and desires a change of your life. Therefore, pray that you may have the strength to change your life. Thank you for having responded to my call."

June 25, 1990

"Dear children!

Today I desire to thank you for all your sacrifices and for all your prayers, I am blessing you with my special motherly blessing. I invite yo all to decide for God, so that from day to day you will discover His will in prayer. I desire, dear children, to call all of you to a full conversion so that joy will be in your hearts. I am happy that you are here today in such great numbers. Thank you for having responded to my call."

July 25, 1990

"Dear children!

Today I invite you to peace. I have come her as the Queen of Peace and I desire to enrich you with my motherly peace. Dear children, I love you and I desire to bring all of you to the peace which only God gives and which enriches every heart. I invite you to become carriers and witnesses of my peace in this unpeaceful world. Let peace reign in the whole world which is without peace and longs for peace. I bless you with my motherly blessing. Thank you for having responded to my call."

August 25, 1990

"Dear children!

I desire to invite you to take with seriousness and put into practice the messages which I am giving you. You know, little children, that I am with you and I desire to lead you along the same path to heaven, which is beautiful for those who discover it in prayer. Therefore, little children, do not forget that those messages which I am giving you have to be put into your everyday life in order that you might be able to say: 'There, I have taken the messages and tried to live them.' Dear children, I am protecting you before the heavenly Father by my own prayer. Thank you for having responded to my call."

September 25, 1990

"Dear children!

I invite you to pray with the heart in order that your prayer may be a conversation with God. I desire each one of you to dedicate more time to God. Satan is strong and wants to destroy and deceive you in many ways. Therefore, dear children, pray every day that your life will be good for yourselves and for all those you meet. I am with you and I am protecting you even though Satan wishes to destroy my plans and to hinder the desires which the Heavenly Father wants to realize here. Thank you for having responded to my call."

October 25, 1990

"Dear children!

Today I call you to pray in a special way that you offer up sacrifices and good deeds for peace in the world. Satan is strong and with all his strength, desires to destroy the peace which comes from God. Therefore, dear children, pray in a special way with me for peace. I am with you and I desire to help you with my prayers and I desire to guide you on the path of peace. I bless you with my motherly blessing. Do not forget to live the messages of peace. Thank you for having responded to my call."

November 25, 1990

"Dear children!

Today I invite you to do works of mercy with love and out of love for me and for your and my brothers and sisters. Dear children, all that you do for others, do it with great joy and humility towards God. I am with you and day after day I offer your sacrifices and prayers to God for the salvation of the world. Thank you for having responded to my call."

December 25, 1990

"Dear children!

Today I invite you in a special way to pray for peace. Dear children, without peace you cannot experience the birth of the little Jesus neither today nor in your daily lives. Therefore, pray the Lord of Peace that He may protect you with His mantle and that He may help you to comprehend the greatness and the importance of peace in your heart. In this way you shall be able to spread peace from your heart throughout the whole world. I am with you and I intercede for you before God. Pray, because Satan wants to destroy my plans of peace. Be reconciled with one another and by means of your lives help peace reign in the whole earth. Thank you for having responded to my call."

January 25, 1991

"Dear children!

Today, like never before, I invite you to prayer. Let your prayer be a prayer for peace. Satan is strong and desires to destroy not only human life, but also nature and the planet on which you live. Therefore, dear children, pray that through prayer you can protect yourselves with God's blessing of peace. God has sent me among you so that I may help you. If you so wish, grasp for the rosary. Even the rosary alone can work miracles in the world and in your lives. I bless you and I remain with you for as long as it is God's will. Thank you for not betraying my presence here and I thank you because your response to serving the good and the peace."

February 25, 1991

"Dear children!

Today, I invite you to decide for God, because distance from God is the fruit of the lack of peace in your hearts. God is only peace. Therefore, approach Him through your personal prayer, and then live peace in your hearts and in this way peace will flow from your heart like a river into the whole world. Do not talk about peace, but make peace. I am blessing each of you and each good decision of yours. Thank you for having responded to my call."

March 25, 1991

"Dear children!

Again today I invite you to live the passion of Jesus in prayer, and in union with Him. Decide to give more time to God who gave you these days of grace. Therefore, dear children, pray and in a special way renew the love for Jesus in your hearts. I am with you and I accompany you with my blessing and my prayers. Thank you for having responded to my call."

April 25, 1991

"Dear children!

Today I invite you all so that your prayer be prayer with the heart. Let each of you find time for prayer so that in prayer you discover God. I do not desire you to talk about prayer, but to pray.

Let your every day be filled with prayer of gratitude to God for life and for all that you have. I do not desire your life to pass by in words but that you glorify God with deeds. I am with you and I am grateful to God for every moment spent with you. Thank you for having responded to my call."

May 25, 1991

"Dear children!

Today I invite all of you who have heard my message of peace to realize it with seriousness and with love in your life. There are many who think that they are doing a lot by talking about the messages, but do not live them. Dear children, I invite you to life and to change all the negative in you, so that it all turns into the positive and live. Dear children, I am with you and I desire to help each of you to live and by living, to witness the good news. I am here, dear children, to help you and to lead you to heaven, and in heaven is the joy through which you can already live heaven now. Thank you for having responded to my call!"

June 25, 1991

"Dear children!

Today on this great day which you have given to me. I desire to bless all of you and to say: these days while I am with you are days of grace. I desire to teach you and help you to walk the way of holiness. There are many people who do not desire to understand my messages and to accept with seriousness what I am saying. But you I therefore call and ask that by your lives and by your daily living you witness my presence. If you pray, God will help you to discover the true reason for my coming. Therefore, little children, pray and read the Sacred Scriptures so that through my coming you discover the messages in Sacred Scripture for you. Thank you for having responded to my call."

July 25, 1991

"Dear children!

Today I invite you to pray for peace. At this time peace is being threatened in a special way, and I am seeking from you to renew fasting and prayer in your families. Dear children, I desire you to grasp the seriousness of the situation and that much of what will happen depends on your prayers and you are praying a little bit. Dear children, I am with you and I am inviting you to begin to pray and fast seriously as in the first days of my coming. Thank you for having responded to my call."

August 25, 1991

"Dear children!

Today also I invite you to prayer, now as never before when my plan has begun to be realized. Satan is strong and wants to sweep away plans of peace and joy and make you think that my Son is not strong in His decisions. Therefore, I call all of you, dear children to pray and fast still more firmly. I invite you to realize through the secrets I began in Fatima may be fulfilled. I call you, dear children, to grasp the importance of my coming and the seriousness of the situation I want to save all souls and present them to God. Therefore, let us pray that everything I have begun be fully realized. Thank you for having responded to my call."

September 25, 1991

"Dear children!

Today in a special way I invite you all to prayer and renunciation. For now as never before Satan wants to show the world his shameful face by which he wants to seduce as many people as possible onto the way of death and sin. Therefore, dear children, help my Immaculate Heart to triumph in the sinful world. I beseech all of you to offer prayers and sacrifices for my intentions so I can present them to God for that is most necessary. Forget your desires, dear children, and pray for what God desires, and not for that you desire. Thank you for having responded to my call."

November 25, 1991

"Dear children!

This time also I am inviting you to prayer. Pray that you might be able to comprehend what God desires to tell you through my presence and through the messages I am giving you. I desire to draw you ever closer to Jesus and to His wounded heart that you might be able to comprehend the immeasurable love which gave itself for each one of you. Therefore, dear children, pray that from your heart would flow a fountain of love to every person both to the one who hates you and to the one who despises you. That way you will be able through Jesus' love to overcome all the misery in this world of sorrows, which is without hope for those who do not know Jesus. I am with you and I love you with the immeasurable love of Jesus. Thank you for all your sacrifices and prayers. Pray so I might be able to help you still more. Your prayers are necessary to me. Thank you for having responded to my call."

December 25, 1991

"Dear children!

Today in a special way I bring the little Jesus to you, that He may bless you with His blessing of peace and love. Dear children, do not forget that this is a grace which many people neither understand nor accept. Therefore, you who have said that you are mine, and seek my help, give all of yourself. First of all, give your love and example in your families. You say that Christmas is a family feast. Therefore, dear children, put God in the first place in your families, so that he may give you peace and may protect you not only from war, but also in peace protect you not only from war, but also in peace protect you from every satanic attack. When God is with you, you have everything. But when you do not want Him, then you are miserable and lost, and you do not know on whose side you are. Therefore, dear children, decide for God. Then you will get everything. Thank you for having responded to my call."

January 25, 1992

"Dear children!

Today, I am inviting you to a renewal of prayer in your families, so that way every family will become a joy to my Son Jesus. Therefore, dear children, pray and seek more time for Jesus and then you will be able to understand and accept everything, even the most difficult sicknesses and crosses. I am with you and I desire to take you into my heart and protect you, but you have not yet decided. Therefore, dear children, I am seeking for you to pray, so through prayer you would allow me to help you. Pray, my dear little children, so prayer becomes your daily bread. Thank you for having responded to my call."

February 25, 1992

"Dear children!

Today I invite you to draw still closer to God through prayer. Only that way will I be able to help you and to protect you from every attack of Satan. I am with you and I intercede for you with God that He protect you. But I need your prayers and your 'Yes.' You get lost easily in material and human things, and forget that God is your greatest friend. Therefore, my dear little children, draw close to God so He may protect you and guard you from every evil. Thank you for having responded to my call."

March 25, 1992

"Dear children!

Today as never before I invite you to live my messages and to put them into practice in your life. I have come to you to help you and, therefore, I invite you to change your life because you have taken a path of misery, a path of ruin. When I told you: convert, pray, fast, be reconciled, you took these messages superficially. You started to live them and then you stopped, because it was difficult for you. No, dear children, when something is good, you have to persevere in the good and not think: God does not see me, He is not listening, He is not helping. And so you have gone away from God and from me because of your miserable interest. I wanted to create of you an oasis of peace, love and goodness. God want you, with your love and with His help, to do miracles and, thus, give an example. Therefore, here is what I say to you: Satan is playing with you and with your souls and I cannot help you because you are far away from my heart. Therefore, pray, live my messages and then you will see the miracles of God's love in your everyday life. Thank you for having responded to my call."

April 25, 1992

"Dear children!

Today also I invite you to prayer. Only by prayer and fasting can war be stopped. Therefore, my dear little children, pray and by your life give witness that you are mine and that you belong to me, because Satan wishes in these turbulent days to seduce as many souls as possible. Therefore, I invite you to decide for God and He will protect you and show you what you should do and which path to take. I invite all those who have said 'yes' to me to renew their consecration to my Son Jesus and to His Heart and to me so we can take you more intensely as instruments of peace in this unpeaceful world. Medjugorje is a sign to all of you and a call to pray and live the days of grace that God is giving you. Therefore, dear children, accept the call to prayer with seriousness. I am with you and your suffering is also mine. Thank you for having responded to my call."

May 25, 1992

"Dear children!

Today also I invite you to prayer so that through prayer you come still nearer to God. I am with you and I desire to lead you on the path to salvation that Jesus gives you. From day to day, I am nearer to you although you are not aware of it and you do not want to admit that you are only linked to me in a small way with your few prayers. When trials and problems arise, you say, 'O God! O Mother! Where are you?' As for me, I only wait for your 'Yes' to present to Jesus for Him to fill you with His grace. That is why, once more, please accept my call and start to pray in a new way until prayer becomes joy to you. Then you will discover that God is all powerful in your daily life. I am with you and I am waiting for you. Thank you for having responded to my call."

June 25, 1992

"Dear children!

Today I am happy, even if in my heart there is still a little sadness for all those who have started on this path and then have left it. My presence here is to take you on a new path, the path to salvation. This is why I call you, day after day to conversion. But if you do not pray, you can not say that you are on the way to being converted. I pray for you and I intercede to God for peace; first peace in your hearts and also peace around you, so that God may be your peace. Thank you for having responded to my call."

July 25, 1992

"Dear children!

Today also I invite you to prayer, a prayer of joy so that in these sad days no one amongst you may feel sadness in prayer, but a joyful meeting with God His Creator. Pray, little children, to be able to come closer to me and to feel through prayer what it is I desire from you. I am with you and each day I bless you with my maternal blessing so that Our Lord may fill you abundantly with His grace for your daily life. Give thanks to God for the grace of my being able to be with you because I assure you it is a great grace. Thank you for having responded to my call."

August 25, 1992

"Dear children!

Today I desire to tell you that I love you. I love you with my maternal love and I invite you to open yourselves completely to m e so that, through each one of you, I can convert and save this world which is full of sin and bad things. That is why, my dear little children, you should open yourselves completely to me so that I may carry you always further toward the marvelous love of God the Creator who reveals Himself to you from day to day. I am with you and I wish to reveal to you and show you the God who loves you. Thank you for having responded to my call."

September 25, 1992

"Dear children!

Today again I would like to say to you that I am with you also in these troubled days during which Satan wishes to destroy all that my Son Jesus and I are building. He desires especially to destroy your souls. He wants to take you away as far as possible from the Christian life and from the commandments that the Church calls you to live. Satan wishes to destroy everything that is holy in you and around you. This is why, little children, pray, pray, pray to be able to grasp all that God is giving you through my coming. Thank you for having responded to my call."

October 25, 1992

"Dear children!

I invite you to prayer now when Satan is strong and wishes to make as many souls as possible his own. Pray, dear children, and have more trust in me because I am here in order to help you and to guide you on a new path toward a new life. Therefore, dear little children, listen and live what I tell you because it is important for you when I shall not be with you any longer that you remember my words and all that I told you. I call you to begin to change your life from the beginning and that you decide for conversion not with words but with your life. Thank you for having responded to my call."

November 25, 1992

"Dear children!

Today, more than ever, I am calling you to pray. May your life become a continuous prayer. Without love you can not pray. That is why I am calling you to love God, the Creator of your lives, above everything else. Then you will come to know God and will love Him in everything as He loves you. Dear children, it is a grace that I am with you. That is why you should accept and live my messages for your own good. I love you and that is why I am with you, in order to teach you and to lead you to a new life of conversion and renunciation. Only in this way will you discover God and all that which now seems so far away from you. Therefore, my dear children, pray. Thank you for having responded to my call."

December 25, 1992

"Dear children!

I desire to place all of you under my mantel and protect you from all satanic attacks. Today is a day of peace, but in the whole world there is a great lack of peace. That is why I call you all to build a new world of peace with me through prayer. This I can not do without you, and this is why I call all of you with my motherly love and God will do the rest. So, open yourselves to God's plan and to His designs to be able to cooperate with Him for peace and for everything that is good. Do not forget that your life does not belong to you, but is a gift with which you must bring joy to others and lead them to eternal life. May the tenderness of the little Jesus always accompany you. Thank you for having responded to my call."

January 25, 1993

"Dear children!

Today I call you to accept and live my messages with seriousness. These days are the days when you need to decide for God, for peace and for the good. May every hatred and jealously disappear from your life and your thoughts, and may there only dwell love for God and for your neighbor. Thus, and only thus shall you be able to discern the signs of the time. I am with you and I guide you into a new time, a time which God gives you as grace so that you may get to know Him more. Thank you for having responded to my call."

February 25, 1993

"Dear children!

Today I bless you with my motherly blessing and I invite you all to conversion, I wish that each of you decide for a change of life and that each of you works more in the Church not through words and thoughts but through example, so that your life may be a joyful testimony for Jesus. You cannot say that you are converted, because your life must become a daily conversion. In order to understand what you have to do, little children, pray and God will give you what you completely have to do, and where you have to change. I am with you and place you all under my mantle. Thank you for having responded to my call."

March 25, 1993

"Dear children!

Today like never I call you to pray for peace, for peace in your hearts, peace in your families and peace in the whole world, because Satan wants war, wants lack of peace, wants to destroy all which is good. Therefore, dear children, pray, pray, pray. Thank you for responding to my call."

April 25, 1993

"Dear children!

Today I invite you all to awaken you hearts to love. God into nature and look how nature is awakening and it will be a help to you to open your hearts to the love of God, the Creator. I desire you to awaken love in your families so that where there is unrest and hatred, love will reign and when there is love in your hearts then there is also prayer. And, dear children, do not forget that I am with you and I am helping you with my prayer that God may give you the strength to love. I bless and love you with my motherly love. Thank you for having responded to my call."

May 25, 1993

"Dear children!

Today I invite you to open yourselves to God by means of prayer so the Holy Spirit may begin to work miracles in you and through you. I am with you and I intercede before God for each one of you because, dear children, each one of you is important in my plan of salvation. I invite you to be carriers of good and peace. God can give you peace only if you convert and pray. Therefore, my dear little children, pray, pray, pray and do that which the Holy Spirit inspires you. Thank you for having responded to my call."

June 25, 1993

"Dear children!

Today I also rejoice at your presence here. I bless you with my motherly blessing and intercede for each one of you before God. I call you anew to live my messages and to put them into life and practice. I am with you and bless all of you day by day. Dear children, these are special times and, therefore, I am with you to love and protect you; to protect your hearts from Satan and to bring you all closer to the heart of my Son, Jesus. Thank you for having responded to my call."

July 25, 1993

"Dear children!

I thank you for your prayers and for the love you show toward me. I invite you to decide to pray for my intentions. Dear children, offer novenas, making sacrifices wherein you feel the most bound. I want your life to be bound to me. I am your Mother, little children, and I do not want Satan to deceive you for he wants to lead you the wrong way, but he cannot if you do not permit him. Therefore, little children, renew prayer in your hearts, and then you will understand my call and live my desire to help you. Thank you for having responded to my call."

August 25, 1993

"Dear children!

I want you to understand that I am your Mother, that I want to help you and call you to prayer. Only by prayer can you understand and accept my messages and practice them in your life. Read Sacred Scripture, live it, and pray to understand the signs of the times. This is a special time, therefore, I am with you to draw you close to my heart and the heart of my Son, Jesus. Dear little children, I want you to be children of the light and not of the darkness. Therefore, live what I am telling you. Thank you for having responded to my call."

September 25, 1993

"Dear children!

I am your Mother and I invite you to come closer to God through prayer because only He is your peace, your Savior. Therefore, little children, do not seek comfort in material things, but rather seek God. I am praying for you and I intercede before God for each individual. I am looking for your prayers that you accept me and accept my messages as in the first days of the apparitions and only then when you open your hearts and pray will miracles happen. Thank you for having responded to my call."

October 25, 1993

"Dear children!

These years I have been calling you to pray, to live what I am telling you, but you are living my messages a little. You talk, but do not live, that is why little children, this war is lasting so long. I invite you to open yourselves to God and in your hearts to live with God, living the good and giving witness to my messages. I love you and wish to protect you from every evil, but you do not desire it. Dear children, I cannot help you if you do not live God's commandments, if you do not live the Mass, if you do not give up sin. I invite you to be apostles of love and goodness. In this world of unrest give witness to God and God's love, and God will bless you and give you what you seek from Him. Thank you for having responded to my call."

November 25, 1993

"Dear children!

I invite you in this time like never before to prepare for the coming of Jesus. Let little Jesus reign in your hearts and only then when Jesus is your friend will you be happy. It will not be difficult for you either to pray or offer sacrifices or to witness Jesus' greatness in your life because He will give you strength and joy in this time. I am close to you by my intercession and prayer and I love and bless all of you. Thank you for having responded to my call."

December 25, 1993

"Dear children!

Today I rejoice with the little Jesus and I desire that Jesus' joy may enter into every heart. Little children, with the message, I give you a blessing with my Son Jesus, so that in every heart peace may reign. I love you, little children, and I invite all of you to come closer to me by means of prayer. You talk and talk but do not pray. Therefore, little children, decide for prayer. Only in this way will you be happy and God will give you what you seek from Him. Thank you for having responded to my call."

January 25, 1994

"Dear children!

You are all my children. I love you. But, little children, you must not forget that without prayer you cannot be close to me. In these times Satan wants to create disorder in your hearts and in your families. Little children, do not give in. You should not allow him to lead you and your life. I love you and intercede before God for you. Little children, pray. Thank you for having responded to my call."

February 25, 1994

"Dear children!

Today I thank you for your prayers. All of you have helped me so that this war may end as soon as possible. I am close to you and I pray for each one of you and I beg you; pray, pray, pray. Only through prayer can we defeat evil and protect all that Satan wants to destroy in your lives. I am your Mother and I love you all equally, and I intercede for you before God. Thank you for having responded to my call."

March 25, 1994

"Dear children!

Today I rejoice with you and I invite you to open yourselves to me, and become an instrument in my hands for the salvation of the world. I desire, little children, that all of you who have felt the odor of holiness through the messages which I am giving you to carry, to carry it into this world, hungry for God and God's love. I thank you all for having responded in such a number and I bless you all with my motherly blessing. Thank you for having responded to my call."

April 25, 1994

"Dear children!

Today I invite you to decide to pray according to my intention. Little children, I invite each one of you to help my plan to be realized through this parish. now I invite you in a special way, little children, to decide to go along the way of holiness. Only this way will you be close to me. I love you and I desire to conduct you all with me to Paradise. But, if you do not pray and if you are not humble and obedient to the messages which I am giving you. I cannot help you. Thank you for having responded to my call."

May 25, 1994

"Dear children!

I invite you all to have more trust in me and to live my messages more deeply. I am with you and I intercede before God for you but also I wait for your hearts to open up to my messages. Rejoice because God loves you and gives you the possibility to convert every day and to believe more in God the Creator. Thank you for having responded to my call."

June 25, 1994

"Dear children!

Today I rejoice in my heart in seeing you all present here. I bless you and I call you all to decide to live my messages which I give you here. I desire, little children, to guide you all to Jesus because He is your salvation. Therefore, little children, the more you pray the more you will be mine and of my Son, Jesus. I bless you all with my motherly blessing and I thank you for having responded to my call."

July 25, 1994

"Dear children!

Today I invite you to decide to give time patiently for prayer. Little children, you cannot say you are mine and that you have experienced conversion through my messages if you are not ready to give time to God every day. I am close to you and I bless you all. Little children, do not forget that if you do not pray you are not close to me, nor are you close to the Holy Spirit who leads you along the path to holiness. Thank you for having responded to my call."

August 25, 1994

"Dear children!

Today I am united with you in prayer in a special way, praying for the gift of the presence of my most beloved Son in your home country. Pray, little children, for the health of my most beloved Son, who suffers, and whom I have chosen for these times. I pray and intercede before my Son, Jesus, so that the dream that your fathers had may be fulfilled. Pray, little children, in a special way, because Satan is strong and wants to destroy hope in your heart. I bless you. Thank you for having responded to my call."

September 25, 1994

"Dear children!

I rejoice with you and I invite you to prayer. Little children, pray for my intention. Your prayers are necessary to me, through which I desire to bring you closer to God. he is your salvation. God sends me to help you and to guide you towards Paradise, which is your goal. Therefore, little children, pray, pray, pray. Thank you for having responded to my call."

October 25, 1994

"Dear children!

I am with you and I rejoice today because the Most High has granted me to be with you and to teach you and to guide you on the path of perfection. Little children, I wish you to be a beautiful bouquet of flowers which I wish to present to God for the day of All Saints. I invite you to open yourselves and to live, taking the saints as an example. Mother Church has chosen them, that they may be an impulse for your daily life. Thank you for having responded to my call."

November 25, 1994

"Dear children!

Today I call you to prayer. I am with you and I love you all. I am your Mother and I wish that your hearts be similar to my heart. Little children, without prayer, you cannot live and say that you are mine. prayer is joy. Prayer is what the human heart desires. Therefore, get closer, little children, to my Immaculate Heart and you will discover God. Thank you for having responded to my call."

December 25, 1994

"Dear children!

Today I rejoice with you and I am praying with you for peace; peace in your hearts, peace in your families, peace in your desires, peace in the whole world. May the King of Peace bless you today and give you peace. I bless you and I carry each one of you in my heart. Thank you for having responded to my call."

January 25, 1995

"Dear children!

I invite you to open the door of your heart to Jesus as the flower opens itself to the sun. Jesus desires to fill your hearts with peace and joy. You cannot, little children, realize peace if you are not at peace with Jesus. Therefore, I invite you to confession so Jesus may be your truth and peace. So, little children, pray to have the strength to realize what I am telling you. I am with you and I love you. Thank you for having responded to my call."

February 25, 1995

"Dear children!

Today I invite you to become missionaries of my messages, which I am giving here through this place that is dear to me. God has allowed me to stay this long with you and therefore, little children, I invite you to love with love the messages I give and to transmit them to the whole world, so that a river of love flows to people who are full of hatred and without peace. I invite you, little children, to become peace where there is no peace and light where there is darkness, so that each heart accepts the light and the way of salvation. Thank you for having responded to my call."

March 25, 1995

"Dear children!

Today I invite you to live the peace in your hearts and families. There is no peace, little children, where there is no prayer and there is no love, where there is no faith. Therefore, little children, I invite you all, to decide again today for conversion. I am close to you and I invite you all, little children, into my embrace to help you, but you do not want it and in this way, Satan is tempting you, and in the smallest thing, your faith disappears. This is why, little children, pray and through prayer, you will have blessing and peace. Thank you for having responded to my call."

April 25, 1995

"Dear children!

Today I call you to love. Little children, without love you can neither live with God nor with brother. Therefore, I call all of you to open your hearts to the love of God that is so great and open to each one of you. God, out of love for man, has sent me among you to show you the path of salvation, the path of love. If you do not first love God, then you will neither be able to love neighbor nor the one you hate. Therefore, little children, pray and through prayer you will discover love. Thank you for having responded to my call."

May 25, 1995

"Dear children!

I invite you, little children, to help me through your prayers so that as many hearts as possible come close to my Immaculate Heart. Satan is strong and with all his forces wants to bring closer the most people possible to himself and to sin. That is why he is on the prowl to snatch more every moment. I beg you, I am your Mother and I love you and that is why I wish to help you. Thank you for having responded to my call."

June 25, 1995

"Dear children!

Today I am happy to see you in such great numbers, that you have responded and have come to live my messages. I invite you, little children, to be my joyful carriers of peace in this troubled world. Pray for peace so that as soon as possible a time of peace, which my heart waits impatiently for, may reign. I am near to you, little children, and intercede for every one of you before the Most High. I bless you with my motherly blessing. Thank you for having responded to my call."

July 25, 1995

"Dear children!

Today I invite you to prayer because only in prayer can you understand my coming here. The Holy Spirit will enlighten you to understand that you must convert. Little children, I wish to make of you a most beautiful bouquet prepared for eternity but you do not accept the way of conversion, the way of salvation that I am offering you through these apparitions. Little children, pray, convert your hearts and come closer to me. May good overcome evil. I love you and bless you. Thank you for having responded to my call."

August 25, 1995

"Dear children!

Today I invite you to prayer. Let prayer be life for you. A family cannot say that it is in peace if it does not pray. Therefore, let you r morning begin with morning prayer, and the evening end with thanksgiving. Little children, I am with you, and I love you and I bless you and I wish for everyone of you to be in my embrace. You cannot be in my embrace if you are not ready to pray every day. Thank you for having responded to my call."

September 25, 1995

"Dear children!

Today I invite you to fall in love with the Most Holy Sacrament of the Altar. Adore Him, little children, in you Parishes and in this way you will b united with the entire world. Jesus will become your friend and you will not talk of Him like someone whom you barely know. Unity with Him will be a joy for you and you will become witnesses to the love of Jesus that He has for every creature. Little children, when you adore Jesus you are also close to me. Thank you for having responded to my call."

October 25, 1995

"Dear children!

Today I invite you to go into nature because there you will meet God the Creator. Today I invite you, little children, to thank God for all that He gives you. In thanking Him you will discover the Most High and all the goods that surround you. Little children, God is great and His love for every creature is great. Therefore, pray to be able to understand the love and goodness of God. In the goodness and the love of God the Creator, I also am with you as a gift. Thank you for having responded to my call."

November 25, 1995

"Dear children!

Today I invite you that each of you begin again to love, in the first place, God who saved and redeemed each of you, and then brothers and sisters in your proximity. Without love, little children, you cannot grow in holiness and cannot do good deeds. Therefore, little children, pray without ceasing that God reveals His love to you. I have invited all of you to unite yourselves with me and to love. Today I am with you and invite you to discover love in your hearts and in the families. For God to live in your hearts, you must love. Thank you for having responded to my call."

December 25, 1995

"Dear children!

Today I also rejoice with you and I bring you little Jesus, so that He may bless you. I invite you, dear children, so that your life may be united with Him. Jesus is the King of Peace and only He can give you the peace that you seek. I am with you and I present you to Jesus in a special way, now in this new time in which one should decide for Him. This time is the time of grace. Thank you for having responded to my call."

January 25, 1996

"Dear children!

Today I invite you to decide for peace. Pray that God gives you the true peace. Live peace in your hearts and you will understand, dear children, that peace is the gift of God. Dear children, without love you cannot live peace. The fruit of peace is love and the fruit of love is forgiveness. I am with you and I invite all of you, little children, that before all else forgive in the family and then you will be abel to forgive others. Thank you for having responded to my call."

February 25, 1996

"Dear children!

Today I invite you to conversion. This is the most important message that I have given you here. Little children, I wish that each of you become a carrier of my messages. I invite you, little children, to live the messages that I have given you over these years. This time is a time of grace. Especially now, when the CHurch also is inviting you to prayer and conversion. I also, little children, invite you to live my messages that I have given you during the time since I appear here. Thank you for having responded to my call."

March 25, 1996

"Dear children!

I invite you to decide again to love God above all else. In this time when due to the spirit of consumerism one forgets that it means to love and to cherish true values, I invite you again, little children, to put God in the first place in your life. Do not let Satan attract you through material things but little children, decide for God who is freedom and love. Choose life and not death of the soul, little children, and in this time when you meditate upon the suffering and death of Jesus I invite you to decide for life which blossomed through the Resurrection, and that your life may be renewed today through conversion that shall lead you to eternal life. Thank you for having responded to my call."

April 25, 1996

"Dear children!

Today I invite you again to put prayer in the first place in your families. Little children, when God is in the first place, then you will, in all that you do, seek the will of God. In this way you daily conversion will become easier. Little children, seek with humility that which is not in order in your hearts, and you shall understand what you have to do. Conversion will become a daily duty that you will do with joy. Little children, I am with you, I bless you all and I invite you to become my witnesses by prayer and personal conversion. Thank you for having responded to my call."

May 25, 1996

"Dear children!

Today I wish to thank you for all you prayers and sacrifices that you, during this month which is consecrate to me, have offered to me. Little children, I also wish that you all become active during this time that is through my connected to heaven in a special way. Pray in order to understand that you all, through your life and your example, ought to collaborate in the work of salvation. Little children, I wish that all people convert and see me and my Son, Jesus, in you. I will intercede for you and help you to become the light. In helping the other, your soul will also find salvation. Thank you for having responded to my call."

June 25, 1996

"Dear children!

Today I thank you for all the sacrifices you have offered me these days. Little children, I invite you to open yourselves to me and to decide for conversion. Your hearts, little children, are still not completely open to me and therefore, I invite you again to open to prayer so that in prayer the Holy Spirit will help you, that your hearts become of flesh and not of stone. Little children, thank you for having responded to my call and for having decided to walk with me toward holiness."

July 25, 1996

"Dear children!

Today I invite you to decide every day for God. Little children, you speak much about God, but you witness little with your life. Therefore, little children, decide for conversion, that your life may be true before God, so that in the truth of your life you witness the beauty God gave you. Little children, I invite you again to decide for prayer because through prayer, you will be able to live the conversion. Each one of you shall become in the simplicity, similar to a child which is open to the love of the Father. Thank you for having responded to my call."

August 25, 1996

"Dear children!

Listen, because I wish to speak to you and to invite you to have more faith and trust in God, who love you immeasurably. Little children, you do not know how to live in the grace of God, that is why I call you all anew, to carry the word of God in your heart and in thoughts. Little children, place the Sacred Scripture in the visible place in your family, and read and live it. Teach your children, because if you are not an example to them, children depart into godlessness. Reflect and pray and then God will be born in you heart and your hear will be joyous. Thank you for having responded to my call."

September 25, 1996

"Dear children!

Today I invite you to offer your crosses and suffering for my intentions. Little children, I am your MOther and I wish to help you by seeking for you the grace from God. Little children, offer your sufferings as a gift to God so they become a most beautiful flower of joy. That is why, little children, pray that you may understand that suffering can become joy and the cross the way of joy. Thank you for having responded to my call."

October 25, 1996

"Dear children!

Today I invite you to open yourselves to God the Creator, so that He changes you. Little children, you are dear to me. I love you all and I call you to be closer to me and that your love towards my Immaculate Heart be more fervent. I wish to renew you and lead you with my Heart to the Heart of Jesus, which still today suffers for you and calls you to conversion and renewal. Through you, I wish to renew the world. Comprehend, little children, that you are today the salt of the earth and the light of the world. Little children, I invite you and I love you and in a special way implore: Convert!" Thank you for having responded to my call."

November 25, 1996

"Dear children!

Today, again, I invite you to pray, so that through prayer, fasting and small sacrifices you amy prepare yourselves for the coming of Jesus. May this time, little children, be a time of grace for you. use every moment and do good, for only in this way will you feel the birth of Jesus in your hearts. If with your life you give an example and become a sign of God's love, joy will prevail in the hearts of men. Thank you for having responded to my call."

December 25, 1996

"Dear children!

Today I am with you in a special way, holding little Jesus in my lap and I invite you, little children, to open yourselves to His call. He calls you to joy. Little children, joyfully live the messages of the Gospel, which I am repeating in the time since I am with you. Little children, I am your Mother and I desire to reveal to you the God of love and the God of peace. I do not desire for your life to be in sadness but that it be realized in joy for eternity, according to the Gospel. Only in this way will your life have meaning. Thank you for having responded to my call."

January 25, 1997

"Dear children!

I invite you to reflect about your future. You are creating a new world without God, only with your own strength an that is why you are unsatisfied and without joy in the heart. THis time is my time and that is why, little children, I invite you again to pray. When you find unity with God, you will feel hunger for the word of God and your heart, little children, will overflow with joy. you will witness God's love wherever you are. I bless you and I repeat to you that I am with you to help you. Thank you for having responded to my call."

February 25, 1997

"Dear children!

Today I invite you in a special way to open yourselves to God the Creator and to become active. I invite you, little children, to see at this time who needs your spiritual or material help. By your example, little children, you will be the extended hands of God, which humanity is seeking. Only in this way will you understand, that you are called to witness and to become joyful carriers of God's words and of His love. Thank you for having responded to my call."

March 25, 1997

"Dear children!

Today, in a special way, I invite you to take the cross in the hands and to meditate on the wounds of Jesus. Ask of Jesus to heal your wounds, which you, dear children, during your life sustained because of your sins or the sins of your parents. Only in this way, dear children, you will understand that the world is in need of healing of faith in God the Creator. By Jesus' passion and death on the cross, you will understand that only through prayer you, too, can become true apostles of faith; when, in simplicity and prayer, you live faith which is a gift. Thank you for having responded to my call."

April 25, 1997

"Dear children!

Today I call you to have your life be connected with God the Creator, because only in this way will your life have meaning and you will comprehend that God is love. God sends me to you out of love, that I may help you to comprehend that without Him there is no future or joy and, above all, there is no eternal salvation. Little children, I call you to leave sin and to accept prayer at all times, that you may in prayer come to know the meaning of your life. God gives Himself to him who seeks Him. Thank you for having responded to my call."

May 25, 1997

"Dear children!

Today I invite you to glorify God and for the Name of God to be holy in your hearts and in your life. Little children, when you are in the holiness of God, He is with you and gives you peace and joy which come from God only through prayer. That is why, little children, renew prayer in your families an your heart will glorify the holy Name of God and heaven will reign in your heart. I am close to you and I intercede for you before God. Thank you for having responded to my call."

June 25, 1997

"Dear children!

Today I am with you in a special way and I bring you my motherly blessing of peace. I pray for you and I intercede for yo before God, so that you may comprehend that each of you is a carrier of peace. You cannot have peace if your heart is not at peace with God. That is why, little children, pray, pray, pray, because prayer is the foundation of your peace. Open your heart and give time to God so that He will be your friend. When true friendship with God is realized, no storm can destroy it. Thank you for having responded to my call."

16th Year Anniversary

July 25, 1997

"Dear children!

Today I invite you to respond to my call to prayer. I desire, dear children, that during this time you find a corner for personal prayer. I desire to lead you toward prayer with the heart. Only in this way will you comprehend that your life is empty without prayer. you will discover the meaning of your life when you discover GOD in prayer. That is why, little children, open the door of your heart and you will comprehend that prayer is joy without which you cannot live. Thank you for having responded to my call."

August 25, 1997

"Dear children!

God give me this time as a gift to you, so that I may instruct and lead you on the path of salvation. Dear children, now you do not comprehend this grace, but soon a time will come when you will lament for these messages. That is why, little children, live all of the words which I have given you through this time of grace and renew payer, until prayer becomes a joy to you. Especially, I call all those who have consecrated themselves to my Immaculate Heart to become an example to others. I call all priests and religious brothers and sisters to pray the rosary and to teach others to pray. The rosary, little children, is especially dear to me. Through the rosary open your heart to me and I am able to help you. Thank you for having responded to my call."

September 25, 1997

"Dear children!

Today I call you to comprehend that without love you cannot comprehend that God needs to be in th first place in your life. That is why, little children, I call you all to love, not with a human but with God's love. In this way, your life will be more beautiful and without an interest. You will comprehend that God gives Himself to you in the simples way out of love. Little children, so that you may comprehend my words which I give you out of love, pray, pray, pray and you will be able to accept others with love and to forgive all who have done evil to you. Respond with prayer, prayer is the fruit of love towards God the Creator. Thank you for having responded to my call."

October 25, 1997

"Dear children!

Also today I am with you and I call all of you to renew yourselves by living my messages. Little children, may prayer be life for you and may you be an example to others. Little children, I desire for you to become carriers of peace and of God's joy to today's world, without peace. That is why, little children, pray! pray! pray! I am with you and I bless you with my motherly peace. Thank you for having responded to my call."

November 25, 1997

"Dear children!

Today I invite you to comprehend your Christian vocation. Little children, I led and am leading you through this time of grace, that you may become conscious of your Christian vocation. Holy Martyrs died witnessing—'I am Christian and love God over everything.' Little children, today also I invite you to rejoice and be joyful Christians, responsible and conscious that God called you in a special way to be joyfully extended hands toward those who do not believe, and that through the example of your life, they may receive faith and love for God. Therefore, pray, pray, pray that your heart may open and be sensitive for the Word of God. Thank you for having responded to my call."

December 25, 1997

"Dear children!

Also today I rejoice with you and I call you to the good. I desire that each of you reflect and carry peace in your heart and say: 'I want to put God first in my life.' In this way, little children, each of you will become holy. Little children, tell everyone, 'I want (the) good for you,' an they will respond with the good. And, little children, good will come to dwell in the heart of each man. Little children, tonight I bring to you the good of my Son who have His life to save you. That is why, little children, rejoice and extend your hands to Jesus who is only good. Thank you for having responded to my call."

January 25, 1998

"Dear children!

Today again I call all of you to prayer. Only with prayer, dear children, will your heart change, become better, and be more sensitive to the Word of God. Little children, do not permit Satan to pull you apart and to do with you what he wants. I call you to be responsible and determined and to consecrate each day to God in prayer. May Holy Mass, little children, be not a habit for you, but life. By living Holy mass each day, you will feel the need for holiness and you will grow in holiness.

I am close to you and intercede before God for each of you, so that He may give you strength to change your heart. Thank you for having responded to my call."

February 25, 1998

"Dear children!

Also today I am with you and I, again, call all of you to come closer to me through your prayers. In a special way, I call you to renunciation in this time of grace. Little children, meditate on and live, through your little sacrifices, the passion and death of Jesus for each of you. Only if you come closer to Jesus will you comprehend the immeasurable love He has for each of you. Through prayer and your renunciation you will become more open to the gift of faith and love towards the Church and the people who are around you. I love you and bless you. Thank you for having responded to my call."

March 25, 1998

"Dear children!

Also today I call you to fasting and renunciation. Little children, renounce that which hinders you from being closer to Jesus. In a special way I call you: Pray, because only through prayer will you be able to overcome your will and discover the will of God even in the smallest things. By your daily life, little children, you will become an example and witness that you live for Jesus or against Him and His will. Little children, I desire that you become apostles of love. By loving, little children, it will be recognized that you are mine. Thank you for having responded to my call."

April 25, 1998

"Dear children!

Today I call you, through prayer, to open yourselves to God as a flower opens itself to the rays of the morning sun. Little children, do not be afraid. I am with you and I intercede before God for each of you so that your heart receives the gift of conversion. Only in this way, little children, will you comprehend the importance of grace in these times and God will become nearer to you. Thank you for having responded to my call."

May 25, 1998

"Dear children!

Today I call you, through prayer and sacrifice, to prepare yourselves for the coming of the Holy Spirit. Little children, this is a time of grace and so, again, I call you to decide for God the Creator. Allow Him to transform and change you. May your heart be prepared to listen to, and live, everything which the Holy Spirit has in His plan for each of you. Little children, allow the Holy Spirit to lead you on the way of truth and salvation towards eternal life. Thank you for having responded to my call."

June 25, 1998

"Dear children!

Today I desire to thank you for living my messages. I bless you all with my motherly blessing and I bring you all before my Son Jesus. Thank you for having responded to my call."

July 25, 1998

"Dear children!

Today, little children, I invite you, through prayer, to be with Jesus, so that through a personal experience of prayer you may be able to discover the beauty of God's creatures. You cannot speak or witness about prayer, if you do not pray. That is why, little children, in the silence of the heart, remain with Jesus, so that He may change and transform you with His love. This, little children, is a time of grace for you. Make good use of it for your personal conversion, because when you have God, you have everything. Thank you for having responded to my call."

August 25, 1998

"Dear children!

Today I invite you to come still closer to me through prayer. Little children, I am your mother, I love you and I desire that each of you be saved and thus be with me in Heaven. That is why, little children, pray, pray, pray until your life becomes prayer. Thank you for having responded to my call."

September 25, 1998

"Dear children!

Today, I call you to become my witnesses by living the faith of your fathers. Little children, you see signs and messages and do not see that, with every morning sunrise, God calls you to convert and to return to the way of truth and salvation. You speak much, little children, but you work little on your conversion. That is why, convert and start to live my messages, not with your words but with your life. In this way, little children, you will have the strength to decide for the true conversion of the heart. Thank you for having responded to my call."

October 25, 1998

"Dear children!

Today I call you to come closer to my Immaculate Heart. I call you to renew in your families the fervor of the first days when I called you to fasting, prayer and conversion. Little children, you accepted my messages with open hearts, although you did not know what prayer was. Today, I call you to open yourselves completely to me so that I may transform you and lead you to the heart of my son Jesus, so that He can fill you with His love. Only in this way, little children, will you find true peace - the peace that only God gives you. Thank you for having responded to my call."

November 25, 1998

"Dear children!

Today I call you to prepare yourselves for the coming of Jesus. In a special way, prepare your hearts. May holy Confession be the first act of conversion for you and then, dear children, decide for holiness. May your conversion and decision for holiness begin today and not tomorrow. Little children, I call you all to the way of salvation and I desire to show you the way to Heaven. That is why, little children, be mine and decide with me for holiness. Little children, accept prayer with seriousness and pray, pray, pray. Thank you for having responded to my call."

December 25, 1998

"Dear children!

In this Christmas joy I desire to bless you with my blessing. In a special way, little children, I give you the blessing of little Jesus. May He fill you with His peace. Today, little children, you do not have peace and yet you yearn for it. That is why, with my son Jesus, on this day I call you to pray, pray, pray, because without prayer you do not have joy or peace or a future. Yearn for peace and seek it, for God is true peace. Thank you for having responded to my call."

January 25, 1999

"Dear children!

I again invite you to prayer. You have no excuse to work more because nature still lies in deep sleep. Open yourselves in prayer. Renew prayer in your families. Put Holy Scripture in a visible place in your families, read it, reflect on it and learn how God loves His people. His love shows itself also in present times because He sends me to call you upon the path of salvation. Thank you for having responded to my call."

February 25, 1999

"Dear children!

Also today I am with you in a special way contemplating and living the passion of Jesus in my heart. Little children, open your hearts and give me everything that is in them: joys, sorrows and, even the smallest pain, that I may offer them to Jesus; so that with His immeasurable love, He may burn and transform your sorrows into the joy of His resurrection. That is why, I now call you in a special way, little children, for your hearts to open to prayer, so that through prayer you may become friends of Jesus. Thank you for having responded to my call."

March 25, 1999

"Dear children!

I call you to prayer with the heart. In a special way, little children, I call you to pray for conversion of sinners, for those who pierce my heart and the heart of my Son, Jesus with the sword of hatred and daily blasphemies. Let us pray, little children, for all those who do not desire to come to know the love of God, even though they are in the Church. Let us pray that they convert, so that the Church may resurrect in love. Only with love and prayer, little children, can you live this time which is given to you for conversion. Place God in the first place, then the risen Jesus will become your friend. Thank you for having responded to my call."

April 25, 1999

"Dear children!

Also today I call you to prayer. Little children, be joyful carriers of peace and love in this peaceless world. By fasting and prayer, witness that you are mine and that you live my messages. Pray and seek! I am praying and interceding for you before God that you convert; that your life and behavior always be Christian. Thank you for having responded to my call."

May 25, 1999

"Dear children!

Also today I call you to convert and to more firmly believe in God. Children, you seek peace and pray in different ways, but you have not yet given your hearts to God for Him to fill them with His love. So, I am with you to teach you and to bring you closer to the love of God. If you love God above all else, it will be easy for you to pray and to open your hearts to Him. Thank you for having responded to my call."

June 25, 1999

"Dear children!

Today I thank you for living and witnessing my messages with your life. Little children, be strong and pray so that prayer may give you strength and joy. Only in this way will each of you be mine and I will lead you on the way of salvation. Little children, pray and with your life witness my presence here. May each day be a joyful witness for you of God's love. Thank you for having responded to my call."

July 25, 1999

"Dear children!

Also today I rejoice with you and I call you all to prayer with the heart. I call all of you, little children, to give thanks to God here with me for the graces which He gives to you through me. I desire for you to comprehend that I want to realize here, not only a place of prayer but also a meeting of hearts. I desire for my Jesus' and your heart to become one heart of love and peace. That is why, little children, pray and rejoice over everything that God does here, despite that Satan provokes quarrels, Jesus is the way of love. Thank you for having responded to my call."

August 25, 1999

"Dear children!

Also today I call you to give glory to God the Creator in the colors of nature. He speaks to you also through the smallest flower about His beauty and the depth of love with which He has created you. Little children, may prayer flow from your hearts like fresh water from a spring. May the wheat fields speak to you about the mercy of God towards every creature. That is why, renew prayer of thanksgiving for everything He gives you. Thank you for having responded to my call."

September 25, 1999

"Dear children!

Today again I call you to become carriers of my peace. In a special way, now when it is being said that God is far away, He has truly never been nearer to you. I call you to renew prayer in your families by reading the Sacred Scripture and to experience joy in meeting with God who infinitely loves His creatures. Thank you for having responded to my call."

October 25, 1999

"Dear children!

Do not forget: this is a time of grace; that is why, pray, pray, pray! Thank you for having responded to my call."

November 25, 1999

"Dear children!

Also today I call you to prayer. In this time of grace, may the cross be a sign-post of love and unity for you through which true peace comes. That is why, little children, pray especially at this time that little Jesus, the Creator of peace, may be born in your hearts. Only through prayer will you become my apostles of peace in this world without peace. That is why, pray until prayer becomes a joy for you. Thank you for having responded to my call."

December 25, 1999

"Dear children!

This is the time of grace. Little children, today in a special way with little Jesus, whom I hold in my embrace, I am giving you the possibility to decide for peace. Through your 'yes' for peace and your decision for God, a new possibility for peace is opened. Only in this way, little children, this century will be for you a time of peace and well-being. Therefore, put little newborn Jesus in the first place in your life and He will lead you on the way of salvation. Thank you for having responded to my call."

January 25, 2000

"Dear children!

I call you, little children, to pray without ceasing. If you pray, you are closer to God and He will lead you on the way of peace and salvation. That is why I call you today to give peace to others. Only in God is there true peace. Open your hearts and become those who give a gift of peace and others will discover peace in you and through you and in this way you will witness God's peace and love which He gives you. Thank you for having responded to my call."

February 25, 2000

"Dear children!

Wake up from the sleep of unbelief and sin, because this is a time of grace which God gives you. Use this time and seek the grace of healing of your heart from God, so that you may see God and man with the heart. Pray in a special way for those who have not come to know God's love, and witness with your life so that they also can come to know God and His immeasurable love. Thank you for having responded to my call."

March 25, 2000

"Dear children!

Pray and make good use of this time, because this is a time of grace. I am with you and I intercede for each one of you before God, for your heart to open to God and to God's love. Little children, pray without ceasing, until prayer becomes a joy for you. Thank you for having responded to my call."

April 25, 2000

"Dear children!

Also today I call you to conversion. You are concerned too much about material things and little about spiritual ones. Open your hearts and start again to work more on your personal conversion. Decide everyday to dedicate time to God and to prayer until prayer becomes a joyful meeting with God for you. Only in this way will your life have meaning and with joy you will contemplate eternal life. Thank you for having responded to my call."

May 25, 2000

"Dear children!

I rejoice with you and in this time of grace I call you to spiritual renewal. Pray, little children, that the Holy Spirit may come to dwell in you in fullness, so that you may be able to witness in joy to all those who are far from faith. Especially, little children, pray for the gifts of the Holy Spirit so that in the spirit of love, every day and in each situation, you may be closer to your fellow-man; and that in wisdom and love you may overcome every difficulty. I am with you and I intercede for each of you before Jesus. Thank you for having responded to my call."

June 25, 2000

"Dear children!

Today I call you to prayer. The one who prays is not afraid of the future. Little children do not forget, I am with you and I love you all. Thank you for having responded to my call."

July 25, 2000

"Dear children!

Do not forget that you are here on earth on the way to eternity and that your home is in Heaven. That is why, little children, be open to God's love and leave egoism and sin. May your joy be only in discovering God in daily prayer. That is why, make good use of this time and pray, pray, pray; and God is near to you in prayer and through prayer. Thank you for having responded to my call."

August 25, 2000

"Dear children!

I desire to share my joy with you. In my Immaculate Heart I feel that there are many of those who have drawn closer to me and you, in a special way, carrying the victory of my Immaculate Heart in their hearts by praying and converting. I desire to thank you and to inspire you to work even more for God and His Kingdom with love and the power of the Holy Spirit. I am with you and I bless you with my motherly blessing. Thank you for having responded to my call."

September 25, 2000

"Dear children!

Today I call you to open yourselves to prayer. may prayer become joy for you. Renew prayer in your families and form prayer groups. In this way, you will experience joy in prayer and togetherness. All those who pray and are members of prayer groups are open to God's will in their hearts and joyfully witness God's love. I am with you. I carry all of you in my heart and I bless you with my motherly blessing. Thank you for having responded to my call."

October 25, 2000

"Dear children!

Today I desire to open my motherly heart to you and to call you all to pray for my intentions. I desire to renew prayer with you and to call you to fast which I desire to offer to my Son Jesus, for the coming of a new time—a time of spring. In this Jubilee year many hearts have opened to me and the Church is being renewed in the Spirit. I rejoice with you and I thank god for this gift; and you, little children, I call to pray, pray, pray, until prayer becomes a joy for you. Thank you for having responded to my call."

November 25, 2000

"Dear children!

Today when Heaven is near to you in a special way, I call you to prayer so that through prayer you place God in the first place. Little children, today I am near you and I bless each of you with my motherly blessing so that you have the strength and love for all the people you meet in your earthly life and that you can give God's love. I rejoice with you and I desire to tell you that your brother Slavko has been born into Heaven and intercedes for you. Thank you for having responded to my call."

December 25, 2000

"Dear children!

Today when God granted to me that I can be with you, with little Jesus in my arms, I rejoice with you and I give thanks to God for everything He has done in this Jubilee year. I thank God especially for all the vocations of those who said 'yes' to God completely. I bless you all with my blessing and the blessing of the newborn Jesus. I pray that all of you have joy born in your hearts so that in joy you too carry the joy I have today, in the Child. I bring to you the Savior of your hearts and the One who calls you to the holiness of life. Thank you for having responded to my call."

January 25, 2001

"Dear children!

Today I call you to renew prayer and fasting with even greater enthusiasm until prayer becomes a joy for you. Little children, the one who prays is not afraid of the future and the one who fasts is not afraid of evil. Once again, I repeat to you: only through prayer and fasting also wars can be stopped—wars of your unbelief and fear for the future. I am with you and am teaching you little children: your peace and hope are in God. That is why draw closer to God and put Him in the first place in your life. Thank you for having responded to my call."

February 25, 2001

"Dear children!

This is a time of grace. That is why pray, pray, pray until you comprehend God's love for each of you. Thank you for having responded to my call."

March 25, 2001

"Dear children!

Also today I call you to open yourselves to prayer. Little children, you live in a time in which God gives great graces but you do not know how to make good use of them. You are concerned about everything else, but the least for the soul and the spiritual life. Awaken from the tired sleep of your soul and say yes to God with all your strength. Decide for conversion and holiness. I am with you, little children, and I call you to perfection of your soul and of everything you do. Thank you for having responded to my call."

To order additional copies of this book:
Please complete the form below and send to:

CMJ Marian Publishing, Inc.
P.O. Box 661
Oak Lawn, Illinois 60454
888-636-6799 • 708-636-2995
fax: 708-636-2855 • email: jwby@aol.com

Name _____

Address _____

City _____

State _____ Zip _____

Phone _____

Book name	Quantity	Subtotal

**Messages to the World from
  the Mother of God**

(Price $8.00)	X	=	
_____	X	=	
_____	X	=	
Shipping and handling		=	
+ tax (for Illinois residents only)		=	
		Total =	

Check # _____

☐ Visa ☐ MasterCard Exp. _____

Card # _____

Signature _____